HELP! There's a STOVE in my KITCHEN

ANNABEL FRERE

ACKNOWLEDGEMENTS

In helping you to become a culinary success, besides easy and delicious recipes, I have included my secrets to achieving tasty food, as well as useful tips on how to save time and money on household basics – the buzz being on 'going green' wherever possible.

It's worth your while to read the suggestions given on how to reduce your electricity usage and costs, as every amp counts. The sections on washing up and stain removal will save you hours of manual labour and a lot of money. You won't have to throw away that burnt saucepan, as help is at hand to revive it!

Thanks go to my family and friends, who have been ardent supporters of my culinary experiments. Friends, especially Ianthe, have helpfully given me ideas that have been put to good use in this book. My husband Martin has encouraged me to pursue this interest. Our daughters, Georgina and Victoria, have been enthusiastic with their 'requests' for breakfast, lunch and supper, and have introduced many of their friends to my cooking. They now want the recipes, so here they are, available to everyone to enjoy!

ANNABEL FRERE

Published in 2011 by Struik Lifestyle
(an imprint of Random House Struik (Pty) Ltd)
Company Reg. No. 1966/003153/07
80 McKenzie Street, Cape Town 8001
PO Box 1144, Cape Town, 8000, South Africa

PUBLISHER: Linda de Villiers
MANAGING EDITOR: Cecilia Barfield
EDITOR AND INDEXER: Bronwen Leak
DESIGNER: Beverley Dodd
PHOTOGRAPHER: Warren Heath
FOOD STYLIST: Lisa Clark
FOOD STYLIST'S ASSISTANT: Sarah Dall
PROOFREADER: Gill Gordon

Reproduction: Hirt & Carter Cape (Pty) Ltd
Printing and binding: Tien Wah Press (Pte) Limited, Singapore

ISBN 978-1-77007-937-3

www.imagesofafrica.co.za

IMAGES OF AFRICA
P H O T O   L I B R A R Y

Over 40 000 unique African images available to purchase from our image bank at www.imagesofafrica.co.za

CONTENTS

USEFUL INFORMATION

MEASUREMENTS

To make life simpler, all you need for measuring quantities in this book are:

1 cup = 250 ml
1 Tbsp = 15 ml
1 tsp = 5 ml

CHECK THE WEIGHTS OF:

- meat, shown on the shop packaging;
- vegetables, either shown on the packet or weighed in the shop before buying;
- pasta, which usually comes in 500 g packets, ideal for about 6 people; and
- butter, which is normally available in 250 g or 500 g slabs.
- In general, when doubling quantities, do not double the oil/butter content in the recipes.

SAVING ENERGY IN THE HOME

IN GENERAL

- Check your appliance – if it's over 1 kW then it is hungry for electricity. Use it sparingly.
- Avoid leaving appliances on standby mode – this uses up more electricity than you think. In some households, it can cost an enormous 7 000 electricity units a year. So switch off battery chargers, cellphone chargers, microwaves, computers, TVs, DVD players, decoders, hi-fis, game consoles, rechargeable toothbrushes, etc. However, note that there are some appliances that do need to be powered all the time, such as home-security systems, remote-controlled gates and garage doors.

IN THE KITCHEN
Cooking

- Kettles use a lot of electricity. Save money by putting boiled water into a thermos flask for use later and only boil as much water as you need – filling the kettle wastes electricity.
- However, do use a kettle to boil water for cooking, as it is quicker and uses less energy than a pot on the stove.
- If your stove retains heat well, switch it off before you finish cooking. Also, match the size of the pan or pot with the size of the stove plate where possible.
- Use a microwave to cook, as it is quicker and cheaper. One oven uses the same power as approximately 18 microwaves.
- Check your oven temperature with an oven thermometer – older ovens are often too hot (and will ruin your baking!).
- Don't open the oven door when roasting or baking.
- Cut food into smaller portions before cooking to help it cook faster.
- Make your toast in a toaster, not under the grill.
- Boil a variety of vegetables in one pot to save energy and washing up.
- Roast meat and vegetables at the same time to make the most of your oven.
- How about a barbecue or a candlelight dinner?

Fridge

- Turn down the thermostat on your fridge if it's very high.
- Don't open the door unnecessarily. When you open your fridge door for more than a moment, it loses cold air and uses a lot of electricity to cool down again. So be quick and don't let all that cold air out.
- Defrost your freezer regularly.

- To defrost food, move it from the freezer to the fridge for a few hours instead of using the microwave.
- Do not place hot food in the fridge or the deep freeze. Let it cool down first.
- Ensure that fridge-door seals are in good condition.

Washing

- To save hot water, rinse dishes under the cold tap before putting them into warm soapy water.
- Whenever you use your dishwasher, it's the same as switching on about 120 energy-saving lights, so only use it when there is a full load. Use the economy/30-minute programme whenever possible.
- Keep the filter of your dishwasher clean.
- The same applies to washing machines, so only run the machine with a full load and use the 30-minute programme whenever possible.
- If the weather is good, dry the clothes on a washing line outside.
- Don't put dripping wet clothes into the tumble drier.

LIGHTS

- In many homes, lighting accounts for 17–20 per cent of the electricity bill.
- Use energy-saving bulbs (compact fluorescent lamps or CFLs). They use 80 per cent less electricity than ordinary bulbs and last 6–8 times longer.
- When no one is in the room, switch off the lights.
- Use lighter lampshades for brighter lighting.
- Avoid leaving spotlights on for too long, as they use more electricity than other bulbs.

IN THE BATHROOM

- Water heating accounts for 30–50 per cent of the electricity consumed by an average household.
- Shower instead of bathing, as a shower uses much less water and, therefore, less electricity.
- Save singing for after your shower! Evidence suggests that you spend longer in the shower if you sing!
- A geyser (boiler) blanket will insulate your geyser, preventing heat from escaping.
- Turn the geyser's thermostat down to 60 °C.
- Fix any dripping taps, especially hot water taps.

THE SWIMMING POOL

- The swimming pool filter pump is one of the largest consumers of electricity, so reduce the time you operate your pool pump.
- During winter, you can use the pool filter even less (once every few days), as algae growth is limited.
- Cover your pool – it keeps it cleaner, requiring the filter to run less often.

 This symbol shows you where you can save on electricity in the recipes.

HOUSEHOLD TIPS

Here are some handy tips (many of which are 'eco-friendly' and cheap) for saving time on washing up, removing stains and correcting culinary mistakes. Many of these simply require bicarbonate of soda (bicarb), lemon juice, salt or white vinegar.

SAVE TIME WASHING UP

- To prevent dirt from sticking, always rinse then soak dirty pots, pans, dishes and cutlery in soapy water.
- Add a squirt of lemon juice or white vinegar to the water to help cut through grease and dirt.
- Easily clean any burnt pot or pan by filling it with hot water, adding 1 Tbsp bicarb and a squirt of lemon juice, then boiling it for a few minutes.
- To clean roasting pans, sprinkle the surface with bicarb, then pour on a cup of hot water and a dash of white vinegar. The fizzing action will help remove the baked-on grease.

REMOVE STAINS FROM FABRICS (CLOTHING, FURNITURE AND CARPETS)

- To remove red wine from a carpet, sofa or other fabric, sponge with soda water immediately, sprinkle with salt and leave to dry. Wash or dab off with detergent and water.
- For grease or oil stains, cover the area with flour or cornflour and leave to absorb for a few minutes, then brush it off. For stubborn grease, also sponge over with dishwashing liquid. Wash as normal.

- Remove coffee stains from your carpet by blotting up as much as possible immediately, then mix a little dishwashing liquid with a drop of white vinegar and water. Sponge the area, until the stain lifts, then dab with warm water and dry it with a towel.
- Soak tea stains in milk before washing as normal.
- Remove blood stains by sponging or soaking the fabric in cold water, then washing with detergent.
- For carpets, just cover a greasy stain with flour or cornflour and vacuum after 30 minutes.
- Remove candle wax from a carpet by covering the wax in brown paper and then ironing over the wax until it is absorbed.
- For clothes, remove wax by covering both sides of the fabric with brown paper and ironing over it until the wax is absorbed.
- Lipstick can be removed from clothes by dabbing it with a tiny amount of clear alcohol or spraying it with hairspray, then washing as normal.
- To remove bubblegum, rub over it with a block of ice until the bubblegum gathers in a ball.
- White stains on furniture can be removed by rubbing over the mark with a paste of olive oil and table salt.

CORRECT CULINARY MISTAKES

- If your soup or stew is too salty, add a peeled potato and continue to cook. The potato will absorb some of the salt.
- If a stew or gravy is too oily, skim the fat off the top with a shallow spoon, then add a little lemon juice.
- If melting chocolate becomes too dry, add a little vegetable oil.
- If your tomato dish is too acidic, add a little sugar.
- Some recipes have TIPS to help you out or to assist you to recover from a mistake.

OTHER USEFUL TIPS
- To prevent butter from burning, add a little oil.
- To tenderise meat, marinade (soak) it in buttermilk or plain yoghurt first, preferably overnight, to get the enzymes working.

- To peel tomatoes, first put them in boiling water for a minute, which will split the skins.
- To peel garlic, smash the whole garlic clove first with one hit of a rolling pin – the skin will easily come away.
- To stop salt from clogging up, put a few grains of dry rice in the saltcellar, and for pepper, place a dried pea in the pot.
- To prevent food from boiling over, grease the inside rim of the pot with oil.
- To get rid of fridge smells, put an eggcup filled with bicarb inside the fridge.

USING LEMONS
- Submerging a lemon in hot water will give you more juice.
- Clean marks off countertops with half a lemon dipped in bicarb. Don't use this on marble or steel.
- Bleach stains off chopping boards and plastic containers by rubbing lemon on the spots.
- Clean food smells (garlic, onion, fish, etc.) off your hands and chopping boards with lemon juice.
- Squeeze lemon juice into your vase of roses to make them last longer.
- To brighten white fabrics in the wash, pour ¼ cup lemon juice into the washing machine.
- Clean copper, silver and brass with lemon juice.

USING SALT
- Clean stains off teacups and coffee mugs with a lemon dipped in salt.
- To clean up oven spills (when food boils over onto the oven floor), sprinkle salt on top while it's still hot and wipe it off when cool. This will stop your oven smoking and smelling later.
- Use salt to put out small flames.
- Salt melts ice, which is useful for instant defrosting of freezers, windows, icy doorsteps, etc. Be careful to wash it off any metal surface that may corrode.
- Add salt to water to freshen up a smelly drain.
- Get rid of weeds in paving cracks by sprinkling salt on them.
- Deter ants in their tracks by scattering salt on them.

STOCKING THE PANTRY

If you keep a few basic sauces, packets and cans in your pantry you can rustle up many of the tasty dishes in this book and you can also have an emergency snack at any time. Here are some must haves:

FLAVOURINGS
- black pepper (in a grinder)
- chicken/beef/vegetable stock powder
- dried chillies or chilli sauce
- garlic and herb seasoning
- herbs (mixed, origanum, basil, rosemary, etc.)
- packets of brown or white onion soup
- salt
- soy sauce
- spices (ground cumin, curry powder, fish spice, etc.)
- sweet chilli sauce
- tomato sauce
- wholegrain mustard

GENERAL USE
- bicarbonate of soda
- cake flour
- canned Italian tomatoes
- cooking oil spray
- dried egg noodles
- pastas
- pure lemon juice
- rice
- tomato purée
- tuna
- vegetable oil
- white vinegar

THE MORNING AFTER

Never again will you have to ask how to boil, scramble, poach or fry eggs! It's a good idea to test the egg first to ensure that it hasn't gone rotten before you break it open. Simply fill a jug or any container with cold tap water, lower the egg into the water and let it go. If it sinks, it's OK, but if it floats, it's bad and you should throw it away (whole).

EGGS

Boiled eggs

1. Half-fill a small saucepan with water.
2. Bring to the boil and then lower the egg(s) into the saucepan with a spoon.
3. Start timing straight away: for a soft-boiled egg, boil for 3–4 minutes at sea level or 5 minutes if well above sea level. For a hard-boiled egg, boil for 10 minutes no matter where you are.
4. When the time is up, immediately remove the egg from the water and place it in an egg cup.
5. If you want to use the hard-boiled egg for egg mayonnaise, stuffed eggs or any other dish, plunge the cooked egg into cold water straight away to stop the yolk from blackening inside.

 Use boiled water from the kettle to save energy.

TIP If an egg cracks, add a little vinegar to the water to prevent the egg white from floating out.

Poached eggs

IF YOU HAVE A POACHING PAN

1. Bring a little water to the boil in the bottom of the pan.
2. Add a dash of butter to each of the little bowls for the number of eggs you want to cook.
3. Break the eggshells and gently pour the eggs into the bowls, one per bowl.
4. Put on the lid and steam the eggs until the whites are set and the yolks are cooked to your liking – about 3 minutes for a soft yolk.

IF YOU DON'T HAVE A POACHING PAN

1. Bring a little water to the boil in a small saucepan.
2. When simmering, break the eggshell on the side of the pan and gently pour the egg into the water.
3. Cook for 3–4 minutes. This method will give you a sprawling egg – using a very fresh egg will help contain it, as the raw white is thicker.

Scrambled eggs

Use 1–2 eggs per person. You can scramble as many eggs as you want at once.

1. Break the eggs into a mixing bowl, add a dash of cold water and season with salt and pepper. Whisk with a fork.
2. Put about 2 tsp butter into a saucepan and heat over a moderate heat until the butter melts.
3. Add the egg mixture and stir with a wooden spoon. The eggs will start to get lumpy, which is perfect. Keep stirring while they become thicker and creamy.
4. Remove from the heat before they get too thick and dry, and serve immediately with toast.

TIP For creamier scrambled eggs, stir over a low heat. The eggs will thicken slowly for a longer cooking time.

Variations for serving

Mix in chopped, smoked salmon (for luxury!) or chopped ham, or top with a mixture of chopped tomato and sliced spring onions.

Fried eggs

1. Heat about 1 Tbsp oil or butter in a frying pan over a low heat.
2. Break the eggshell on the side of the pan and, to avoid breaking the yolk, gently pour the egg into the frying pan. You can cook 3 or 4 eggs at the same time depending on the size of the pan. They must not be 'swimming' in egg white!
3. Fry gently until the egg white goes opaque all over, spooning a little of the hot oil or butter over the yolk to cook around it.
4. It is ready when you can lift the egg easily with a spatula and the white is cooked through, with the yolk still orangey and soft.
5. If you prefer a hard yolk, you can flip the egg over to cook for 30 seconds on the other side. Alternatively, put a lid on the frying pan and the yolk will harden.

Microwave eggs

This is for when you are in a real hurry and want a very quick egg on toast.

1. Put the bread in the toaster, as this takes longer than the egg.
2. Simply break 1 egg into a cup. Cover the top of the cup securely with clingfilm and put it in the microwave.
3. Cook on high for about 40 seconds for a soft yolk or 50 seconds for a hard yolk. Be warned that eggs DO EXPLODE in microwaves, which is why you need the clingfilm to be securely in place.

TIP Remember, do not use metal or any fancy gold- or silver-bordered cups in the microwave.

Omelettes

Omelettes can be as easy or as adventurous as you like, depending on your choice of filling. Each omelette will need to be cooked separately, so make sure that the ingredients for the filling are ready to be used. Some ingredients, such as bacon, mushrooms and onion, need to be fried first. Others, such as cheese, ham and tomato, can go straight in, with no pre-cooking.

1. Prepare the filling ingredients. You will need 2–3 Tbsp per omelette. Depending on your choice, fry chopped bacon, mushrooms and onion in butter or oil for 3–4 minutes and set aside. Grate some cheese, and chop some ham and tomato, and set aside.
2. Break 2 eggs into a mixing bowl. Add a dash of milk, season with salt and pepper, and whisk with a fork.
3. Heat a medium frying pan over a moderate heat and add 1 tsp butter to melt over the base.
4. Pour in the egg mixture, which will spread out like a pancake. Cook on one side for about 4 minutes, lifting the edge with a spatula to allow the liquid part on top to run underneath.
5. Sprinkle 2–3 Tbsp of the prepared filling ingredients on half of the omelette and fold over the other half. Cook for a further 1–2 minutes.
6. Serve immediately and begin on the next omelette. The pan will be clean enough (or you can wipe it with a paper towel) for the next one to be cooked.

OAT CRUNCHIES

You can make these at the weekend and keep them in a closed container, ready for healthy weekday breakfasts or snacks.

125 g butter
2 Tbsp honey
½ cup brown sugar
3 cups oats
½ cup raisins
1 Tbsp ground almonds
1 Tbsp mixed seeds (sunflower, sesame, pumpkin) (optional)
a pinch of salt

1. Preheat the oven to 180 °C.
2. Melt the butter, honey and sugar in a large saucepan over a moderate heat (or in a large bowl in the microwave for 1–2 minutes).
3. Mix in the remaining ingredients, coating well with the honey mixture.
4. Transfer the mixture to a 22 cm-square baking tin and press flat.
5. Bake for 20 minutes until golden.
6. Remove from the oven and, after a few minutes, loosen around the edges with a knife and cut into squares while warm. Press down on the crunchies with a spatula or clean kitchen towel to prevent them from crumbling and leave to cool in the baking tin.

MAKES 16

FRITTATAS

A frittata is a cross between a deep omelette and a crustless quiche. Instead of making everyone his or her own omelette, make one substantial frittata. It is delicious for breakfast or lunch, or as an anytime snack. It will keep for a day or two in the fridge.

You can use any combination of 3 or 4 fillings, such as cold meats, vegetables and herbs. Some, such as potato, sausage, broccoli, onion and mushrooms, will need pre-cooking, but others, such as cheese, salami, ham, tomato and peppers, won't. Here are two tasty and easy frittata ideas, each serving 2–3 people. To make a larger frittata, simply double all the ingredients except the oil and remember that the egg will take longer to set.

Spinach and feta frittata

200 g spinach, washed well

4 eggs

⅓ cup milk

salt and pepper to taste

1 Tbsp oil

2 spring onions, trimmed and sliced

1 cup grated Cheddar cheese

½ cup cubed Danish feta cheese

garlic and herb seasoning to taste

1. Wilt the spinach by pouring boiling water over it, then draining it well. Roughly chop – no need to mince.
2. Break the eggs into a mixing bowl and beat with a fork or whisk for 1 minute. Add the milk and season with salt and pepper.
3. Mix in the spinach, spring onions and Cheddar cheese.
4. Heat the oil in a large ovenproof frying pan over a moderate heat. Pour in the egg mixture and crumble the feta on top. Sprinkle with garlic and herb seasoning.
5. Fry slowly for 10–15 minutes, until the egg sets underneath. Loosen around the edges with a spatula and lift up the side to check.
6. Preheat the oven's grill.
7. When the frittata is half cooked, place the pan on the oven rack under the preheated grill (not too close to the grill) and, with the oven door open, grill the egg mixture for 5–10 minutes until set and golden on top.
8. Cut into wedges and serve with tomato and cucumber salsa.

Potato, chorizo/salami and pepper frittata

2 Tbsp oil
1 clove garlic, peeled and
    finely chopped
1 medium potato, peeled and
    thinly sliced
1 cup thinly sliced chorizo/salami
½ red pepper, deseeded and chopped
4 eggs
⅓ cup milk
1 cup grated cheese
salt and pepper to taste

1. Heat the oil in a large frying pan over a moderate heat and gently fry the garlic for a few seconds.
2. Add the potato and chorizo/salami. Fry for 10–12 minutes, turning them over until the potato turns golden brown on both sides. Mix in the red pepper and remove from the heat.
3. Preheat the oven's grill.
4. Break the eggs into a mixing bowl and beat with a fork or whisk for 1 minute. Add the milk and cheese, and season with salt and pepper. Pour this into the potato mix in the frying pan and stir once.
5. Fry slowly over a moderate heat without stirring for about 5 minutes, until the egg sets underneath and around the edges. It will start to look 'rounded' at the edges.
6. Place the pan on the oven rack under the preheated grill (not too close to the grill) and, with the oven door open, grill the egg mixture for about 5 minutes until set and golden on top. Do not overcook, as it will dry out.
7. Cut into wedges and serve with tomato and cucumber salsa.

PANCAKES

These can be made in advance,
folded into quarters and frozen in
sandwich bags for convenience. Simply
defrost and add toppings, such as banana and
caramel, lemon and cinnamon sugar, berries and ice cream,
or cheese, ham and tomato. Or eat them fresh while still warm.

2 eggs
1 cup cake flour
½ cup milk mixed with ½ cup water
oil for frying

1. Break the eggs into a mixing bowl, add the flour and a little of the milk-water mixture. Beat well with a whisk, ensuring a smooth consistency, then gradually whisk in the rest of the milk-water mixture.
2. For the first pancake, spray or wipe a medium frying pan with a little oil to make it reliably non-stick. Pour a further 2–3 drops of oil into the pan, tilting it round so that the oil covers the base, and heat over a high heat. When the oil is hot, pour a ladle of the pancake batter into the pan and swish it around so that it spreads thinly over the bottom.
3. After about 15 seconds, little bubbles will start to form all over, which means that it is time to flip the pancake. You can use a spatula to lift it or, if you're feeling brave, you can flip and catch it.
4. Cook the other side for another 15 seconds and then slide the pancake onto a plate. It should be soft and flexible when done, with golden patterns on one side and small brown dots on the other.
5. Pour a tiny drop of oil into the hot frying pan ready to start the next pancake. When the next pancake is done, slide it on top of the first pancake on the plate and continue making a stack of pancakes until the batter is used up.
6. Serve immediately or allow the pancakes to cool under a clean tea towel, so they don't dry out, before freezing them for use later.

MAKES 6 MEDIUM PANCAKES

BRAN MUFFINS

This mixture needs to rest in the fridge overnight before being used. It takes 5 minutes to combine the ingredients and will keep in the fridge for 2–3 weeks. Just fill up a muffin pan and cook them fresh as needed. Handy for instant, fresh, warm muffins!

1¼ cups cake flour
1¼ tsp bicarbonate of soda
1 cup wheat bran
½ cup brown sugar
1 egg
¼ cup oil
1 cup milk
½ cup raisins (optional)
a pinch of salt
1 tsp vanilla essence

1. Combine all of the ingredients in a mixing bowl and mix well. Chill in the fridge overnight.
2. Preheat the oven to 180 °C.
3. Grease a muffin pan with a little oil and place a large spoonful of muffin mix into each slot, to roughly two-thirds full.
4. Bake for 15 minutes until risen and cooked through. Test by lightly pressing the top of a muffin – it should be firm.

MAKES 12

Other breakfast ideas

Here are a few other ideas for a quick breakfast to get you going:

Anchovy toast: Spread anchovy paste on hot buttered toast.

Bacon roll: Fry 2 or 3 pieces of bacon (per person) in a little oil and use to fill a buttered roll with tomato sauce or sliced banana.

Baked beans on toast: Heat half a can of beans (per person) and put on toast.

Banana, plain yoghurt and honey: This is a very good combination to keep your blood-sugar levels stable for a few hours.

French toast: Mix 1 or 2 eggs with a splash of milk. Soak a piece of bread in the egg mixture and lightly fry in a drop of oil on both sides until golden brown. Serve plain or with bacon and syrup.

Ham and cheese croissant: Fill a croissant with slices of ham and cheese and bake on a baking tray at 180 °C for 10 minutes until the cheese has melted.

SMOOTHIES

Smoothies are quick, refreshing and wholesome. You'll need a blender to whizz all the ingredients together. Each of the combinations below serves 1.

- 1 banana, ½ cup oats or muesli, 1 cup plain yoghurt, ¼ cup fruit juice.
- 1 cup mixed berries (fresh or frozen), ½ cup berry juice, 1 large scoop frozen yoghurt, ice cream or berry sorbet.
- 1 banana, 1 cup plain yoghurt, 1 Tbsp honey, 4 tsp Milo. (Freeze peeled and cut ripe bananas for an icy version.)
- 1 cup strawberries, 1 cup plain yoghurt, 2 tsp honey.

STOMACH LINERS

The following selection of snacks is useful for starters, appetizers, lunches and parties, or as a bite before you go out.

CROSTINI

Italian for 'little toasts', crostini are slices of French bread with savoury toppings, toasted in the oven.

1 long French loaf (baguette)
a little oil for drizzling

Some ideas for toppings:
sliced goat's cheese, pesto and cherry tomatoes
sliced mushrooms and cheese
anchovy paste, sliced tomato and cheese
chopped green pepper, sliced onion and cheese
salami, sliced olives and cheese
ham, sliced tomato and cheese

1. Preheat the oven to 180 °C.
2. Slice the French loaf and lay the pieces out on a baking tray. Drizzle a little oil over each.
3. Bake until the slices are lightly toasted on one side. This will be quick, so keep an eye on them.
4. Turn over the slices and top with your desired topping. Return the tray to the oven for about 5 minutes, until the cheese has melted and the edges of the bread are golden. Remove and serve.

WRAPS

Buy ready-made soft tortillas and fill them with any of the following, ensuring that the contents aren't sloppy with too much sauce:

- **STIR-FRIED CHICKEN** (fry chicken strips in 1 tsp oil and a little soy sauce), sliced avocado, fried bacon (optional), salad/coleslaw and mayonnaise.
- **SLICED COOKED CHICKEN** (boil a deboned chicken breast fillet in a small saucepan with enough water to cover and ½ chicken stock cube or 1 tsp chicken stock powder for 15 minutes, until cooked through), mayonnaise, tomato, fresh coriander and lettuce.
- **STIR-FRIED BEEF** (fry strips of beef in 1 tsp oil and a little soy sauce), mustard mixed with mayonnaise, sliced tomato and salad.
- **FRIED HALLOUMI** (fry fingers of halloumi in a dry frying pan until golden, turning once), sweet chilli sauce and salad.
- **CANNED TUNA** mixed with mayonnaise, chopped cucumber, chopped tomato and salad.
- **SMOKED SALMON**, sliced cucumber and cream cheese.

1. Lay the wrap flat on a board and fill the middle section, top to bottom, with the desired filling.
2. Fold the bottom side up about 2 cm and then fold in the side edges, overlapping one over the other.
3. If packing for lunch, roll the wrap in foil, twisting the top edge so that you know which is the open end.
4. For parties, cut the filled wraps into bite-size pieces and display on a plate with the filling showing.

QUICHE

Preparation

1. Grease a shallow, 20 cm-diameter, round, ovenproof dish or baking tin with a little oil. Preheat the oven to 180 °C and put a baking tray in the centre.

Base

You have a choice of either a crispy, crumbly cheese crust or a traditional pastry base.

CHEESE CRUST
1 cup cake flour
125 g chilled butter, cubed
1 cup finely grated cheese

1. Mix everything together in a blender. Alternatively, in a large mixing bowl rub the flour and butter together with your fingers until it resembles breadcrumbs, and then add the cheese.
2. Press the mixture into the greased dish, covering the base and sides.
3. Chill in the fridge while you prepare the filling.

PASTRY BASE
60 g butter, cubed
1 cup cake flour
a pinch of salt
2 Tbsp cold water
1–2 tsp milk

1. Mix the butter, flour and salt in a blender. Alternatively, in a large mixing bowl rub the butter into the flour and salt with your fingers until it resembles breadcrumbs.
2. Mix in the water to make a ball of dough and then chill for 20 minutes.
3. Dust a board and rolling pin with a little flour and thinly roll out the chilled pastry. It must be slightly larger than the dish. Roll it around the rolling pin to lift it up and line the bottom and just over the sides of the greased dish.
4. Prick the base all over with a fork (to stop it rising while cooking), brush with a little milk and bake on the hot baking tray for 20 minutes. In the meantime, prepare the filling.

Filling

1. Whisk the following ingredients together in a mixing bowl and add your filling:

3 eggs   **1 cup grated cheese**

¾ cup cream cheese or crème fraîche   **a little salt and pepper to taste**

- **ASPARAGUS** – pour the basic filling into the quiche base and place ½ can drained asparagus spears or pieces on top.
- **BILTONG AND BLUE CHEESE** – mix 4–5 Tbsp powdered biltong and 2 tsp soy sauce into the basic filling. Crumble in 1 Tbsp blue cheese and pour into the quiche base.
- **CHORIZO (SPICY SAUSAGE) AND TOMATOES** – pour the basic filling into the quiche base and dot evenly with ¾ cup sliced chorizo and about 10 halved baby tomatoes, pushing some down into the egg mix.
- **HAM AND ONION** – mix 4 slices chopped ham and 1 sliced spring onion into the basic filling. Pour into the quiche base.
- **MUSHROOM, ONION AND THYME** – wash and slice 250 g button mushrooms, and peel and finely chop 1 small onion. Fry the onion and mushroom with 1 tsp garlic and herb seasoning in 1 Tbsp butter for 5 minutes. Mix with the basic filling, add a pinch of thyme and pour into the quiche base.
- **SPINACH AND FETA** – wash and roughly chop 150 g baby spinach leaves. Wilt the spinach by pouring boiling water over it, and then drain well. Mix the spinach and ¼ cup cubed feta cheese with the basic filling. Pour into the quiche base.
- **TUNA OR SALMON** – mix 1 x 170 g can tuna (drained) or salmon (drained, and skin and bones removed) into the basic filling. Pour into the quiche base.

Bake

1. No matter the filling, bake for 45–50 minutes. Allow to rest for 10 minutes before serving.

SERVES 4

TIP For best results, use cream cheese or crème fraîche for the filling and **not** cottage cheese, which tends to separate. You can make your own crème fraîche by mixing equal quantities of cream and sour cream in a jar. Cover and leave to stand at room temperature for 24 hours until thickened, then chill until ready to use.

MARMITE ROLLS

These are so easy and will always be in demand!

1 x 400 g roll frozen puff pastry, thawed at room temperature
2–3 Tbsp Marmite
2 cups grated cheese
a little milk

1. Preheat the oven to 180 °C.
2. Unroll the puff pastry and pat flat with your hands.
3. Spread a thin layer of Marmite over the pastry, leaving 1 cm free along one long edge.
4. Sprinkle the grated cheese on top, leaving the same edge free.
5. Dab a little milk on the free edge and roll up the pastry from the other end, gluing the free edge down to create a long sausage-shaped roll.
6. Brush a little milk over the pastry and slice into roughly 1.5 cm-thin rounds. Lay these flat on a baking tray and bake for 25 minutes until brown.

MAKES ABOUT 20

CHEESE PUFFS

1 cup cake flour
2 tsp baking powder
1 cup grated cheese
1 egg, beaten with a fork
1 cup milk
½ tsp English mustard
a pinch of salt
garlic and herb seasoning for sprinkling

1. Preheat the oven to 200 °C. Grease a muffin pan (for large puffs) or a patty tin (for small puffs) with a little oil.
2. Mix all of the ingredients together until smooth.
3. Fill the slots of the muffin pan or patty tin with the mixture and sprinkle over garlic and herb seasoning.
4. Bake for 12 minutes. Test that they are ready by lightly pressing the top of a puff – it should spring back into shape.

MAKES 8 LARGE OR 12 SMALL

CHEESE STRAWS

1 cup cake flour
60 g butter, cubed
1 cup grated cheese
a pinch of salt
a pinch of pepper
½ tsp English mustard powder
2 Tbsp cold water

1. Preheat the oven to 200 °C. Grease a baking tray with a little oil.
2. Mix the flour, butter, cheese, salt, pepper and mustard in a blender until it resembles breadcrumbs. Alternatively, in a large mixing bowl, rub the flour and butter together with your fingers until it resembles breadcrumbs, and then add the cheese, salt, pepper and mustard.
3. Mix in the water to bind the mixture into a soft dough. Form the dough into a ball with your hands.
4. Roll out the dough on a floured surface into a rectangle about 1 cm thick. Cut into 12 strips, twirl them gently and place them on the greased baking tray.
5. Bake for 15 minutes.

MAKES 12

CRISPY CHEESE TORTILLA

Also known as a quesadilla, this is like a crispy, thin pizza sandwich. Cut it into wedges and share with friends – delicious and simple!

2 soft tortillas
1 cup grated cheese
2 tsp oil
garlic and herb seasoning
  for sprinkling

1. Lay one tortilla flat on a board. Sprinkle the cheese evenly on top and cover with the other tortilla.

2. Heat half of the oil in a frying pan over a moderate heat and gently fry the filled tortilla for 2 minutes until golden underneath. Turn it over, add the remaining oil and fry the other side for about 2 minutes until golden with the cheese melted inside.

3. Remove from the pan, sprinkle with garlic and herb seasoning, cut into wedges and serve hot with tomato salsa and guacamole (see page 38).

SERVES 2

NACHOS WITH CHEESE

1 x 250 g pkt nachos or tortilla chips
1 cup grated cheese
guacamole (see page 38)
sour cream
1 small red bell pepper, chopped
fresh coriander

1. Preheat the oven to 180 °C.
2. Place the chips in a baking dish and sprinkle the cheese over the top.
3. Bake for about 10 minutes until the cheese has melted.
4. Serve with the guacamole and sour cream heaped on top or on the side, and garnish with the bell pepper and coriander.

SERVES 3–4

FRIED HALLOUMI AND CHORIZO

This recipe can be doubled easily. Remember, though, not to double the cooking oil!

1 Tbsp oil
6–8 slices halloumi
1 cup sliced chorizo (spicy sausage)
½ cup sundried tomatoes

1. Heat the oil in a large frying pan over a moderate heat.
2. Place the halloumi and chorizo in the pan and fry gently for 5–10 minutes, turning once so that they are browned on both sides.
3. Add the sundried tomatoes, toss well and remove from the heat. Serve with French bread.

SERVES 2

CHILLI CHICKEN LIVERS

250 g chicken livers, trimmed
1 Tbsp oil
1 cup tomato purée
½ cup water
1 tsp tomato sauce
a few drops of chilli sauce to taste

1. Wash the chicken livers in a sieve under cold running water and roughly chop them.
2. Heat the oil in a small saucepan over a moderate heat and add the livers. Stir constantly to brown them all over.
3. Add the remaining ingredients, using only 5 or 6 drops of the chilli sauce at first.
4. Cook over a moderate heat for 5–7 minutes until the sauce thickens. Taste and adjust the chilli as desired.
5. Serve hot with French bread.

SERVES 2–4

TOAST CUPS

This is a good way of using up slightly stale bread for instant entertaining.

1 loaf bread, sliced
oil for greasing
a little butter

FILLING SUGGESTIONS
scrambled egg topped with halved baby tomatoes
chunky cottage cheese topped with chopped ham and pineapple
chicken livers (see page 33), guacamole (see page 38) or salmon mousse (see page 36)

1. Preheat the oven to 180 °C.
2. Remove the crusts and corners, and flatten the bread slices with your hand to thin them slightly.
3. Grease a muffin pan with oil and press a bread slice into each slot to form a cup with a flat base.
4. Bake for 10–15 minutes until golden and crispy.
5. Remove the toast cups from the muffin pan and put a small slice of butter in each one to melt.
6. Fill with any of the suggested fillings (or something of your own making) and serve as soon as possible to avoid the toast getting soggy.

MAKES AS MANY AS YOU LIKE

NUT AND HERB CHEESE ROULADE

This is a soft cheese shaped into a sausage and covered in nuts and herbs. It is very easy to make and looks good on a platter – or simply spread it on French bread or savoury biscuits for a snack.

½ cup cream cheese
½ cup smooth cottage cheese
salt and pepper to taste
¼ cup pecan nuts
2 Tbsp chopped fresh basil
2 Tbsp chopped fresh parsley
2 Tbsp snipped chives
1 red chilli, deseeded and finely chopped

1. Mix the cheeses until smooth and season with salt and pepper.
2. Put the pecan nuts into a mixing bowl and crush them with the end of a rolling pin, to make crumbs.
3. Cut a 30 cm-square piece of clingfilm and lay it out flat. Sprinkle the herbs, chives, chilli and nuts evenly over it.
4. Place the cheese in a line down the middle of the clingfilm and bring up the sides to roll the cheese in the herb mixture. Encase the cheese in the clingfilm and refrigerate for 1–2 hours.
5. Unroll onto a platter when ready to serve.

SERVES 4–6

SALMON MOUSSE

This can be made a day ahead to ensure it sets well.

1 x 415 g can salmon
1 tsp chicken stock powder or ½ stock cube, crumbled
1 Tbsp (or 1 x 10 g sachet) gelatine
cold water
1 Tbsp mayonnaise
1 Tbsp cream (optional)

1. Drain the liquid from the can of salmon into a cup and mix in the chicken stock powder or cube.

2. Add the gelatine and mix well, then microwave for 45 seconds. Alternatively, bring 2 cm of water to the boil in a saucepan on the stove, stand the cup in the saucepan and stir until the gelatine has completely dissolved. Do not boil. Remove from the heat and allow to cool for 5–10 minutes.

3. Top up with cold water, until the cup is three-quarters full. Set aside.

4. Empty the salmon onto a plate and carefully remove the skin and bones. Put the salmon into a blender and add the stock mixture and mayonnaise. Blitz until fairly smooth, then add cream if using.

5. Pour the mixture into a serving bowl or jelly mould and allow to set in the fridge for at least 4 hours or overnight.

6. If you have made the mousse in a jelly mould, turn it out onto a plate before serving with sliced cucumber and Melba toast or French bread.

SERVES 4

DIPS

Serve these dips with a selection of crudités (sliced raw veggies), such as carrot, cucumber, celery, green and red pepper and baby sweetcorn, as well as broccoli and cauliflower florets.

Yoghurt and goat's milk cheese dip

3 Tbsp goat's milk cheese with herbs
1 cup plain yoghurt
2 spring onions, trimmed and sliced
1 Tbsp finely chopped cucumber
1 clove garlic, peeled and finely chopped

1. In a bowl, mash the goat's milk cheese into the yoghurt.
2. Mix in the remaining ingredients and chill until needed.

Yoghurt and cream cheese dips

A variety of dips can be made using ½ cup plain yoghurt mixed with ½ cup cream cheese or smooth cottage cheese and any of the following:

- 1 tsp Bovril and 1 Tbsp soy sauce
- 1 x 170 g can tuna and a squirt of lemon juice
- 2 Tbsp brown or white onion soup powder
- ½ cup pesto
- 1½ Tbsp tomato sauce and 1 tsp chilli sauce
- 1 Tbsp chutney and 1 tsp curry powder
- 1 Tbsp sweet chilli sauce and 2 Tbsp finely chopped peppadews

Tzatziki

½ cucumber, rinsed
2 cloves garlic, peeled and finely chopped
1 cup thick plain yoghurt
salt and pepper to taste

1. Grate or finely chop the cucumber.
2. In a bowl, combine the cucumber, garlic and yoghurt, and mix well. Season with salt and pepper, and chill until needed.

Guacamole

2 ripe avocados
½ tomato
1 tsp mayonnaise
a dash of soy sauce
a squirt of lemon juice
a few drops of Tabasco to taste

1. Cut the avocado in half lengthways and remove the pip. Scoop the flesh into a bowl and mash with a fork.
2. Grate the tomato over the avocado by holding the tomato skin-side flat on your hand and grating it until you are left with the skin, which you'll then throw away.
3. Add the remaining ingredients and mix well to achieve your preferred consistency – chunky or smooth.

Creamy white bean dip

2 Tbsp oil
2 cloves garlic, peeled and finely chopped
1 x 400 g can butter beans
a squeeze of lemon juice
salt and pepper to taste
2 Tbsp cream cheese

1. Heat the oil in a large frying pan over a fairly low heat and fry the garlic for 2 minutes.
2. Drain the butter beans, keeping the liquid in a cup. Add the beans and half of the liquid to the pan. Mix with the garlic, cover the pan and steam over a low heat for 10 minutes.
3. Pour the mixture into a bowl and mash the beans with a fork, adding more of the liquid if too dry.
4. Add the lemon juice, salt and pepper, and mix in the cream cheese.

Guacamole

Creamy white bean dip

Tzatziki

More tzatziki

CHICKEN LIVER PÂTÉ

60 g butter
1 medium onion, peeled and finely chopped
250 g chicken livers, trimmed and washed
1 clove garlic, peeled and finely chopped
½ tsp dried mixed herbs
2 Tbsp sherry, brandy or port
salt and pepper to taste
fresh sage leaves for garnishing

1. Melt half of the butter in a medium frying pan over a moderate heat and fry the onion until soft.
2. Add the chicken livers, garlic and herbs, and stir-fry for 3–4 minutes. Add the alcohol and simmer until the liquid is reduced to very little. Season with salt and pepper and remove from the heat.
3. Blitz in a blender until fairly smooth and pour into a serving pot.
4. Melt the remaining butter and pour over the pâté. Garnish with fresh sage leaves and chill for at least 2 hours before serving with Melba toast or French bread.

CHILLI PHILLY

1 x 250 g Philadelphia soft cheese or any
**   good-quality cream cheese or feta**
sweet chilli sauce

1. Place the whole cheese on a plate and generously pour over the sweet chilli sauce.

CHICKEN STOCK

It is well worth making real chicken stock from the carcass of a roast chicken, for its taste and health benefits. Making your own stock does, however, use a fair amount of electricity, as it needs to boil for 2–3 hours.

1 chicken carcass
2–3 litres cold water
1 onion, peeled and quartered

1 tomato, quartered
a handful of chopped mixed fresh herbs

1. Put everything in a large saucepan on the stove and bring to the boil.
2. Reduce the heat to very low and simmer for 2–3 hours until reduced.
3. Strain the stock through a colander into a mixing bowl and allow to cool.
4. Store in a jar or any sealed container in the fridge. It can even be frozen for up to 2 months.
5. When a recipe calls for stock made from cubes or powder, use this instead.

MAKES ABOUT 2 CUPS

SIMPLE STOCK SAUCE

This sauce is thinner than white sauce. Use it for pies and chicken dishes.

30 g butter
2 Tbsp cake flour

1¼ cups chicken stock made with ½ chicken stock cube or 2 heaped tsp stock powder and 1¼ cups water

1. Melt the butter slowly in a saucepan over a moderate heat. Mix in the flour and heat gently for 1 minute, stirring occasionally.
2. Remove the pan from the heat and whisk in a little of the stock, ensuring that there are no lumps.
3. Add the rest of the stock gradually, stirring all the time, and then return the pan to the heat. Keep stirring until the sauce thickens and comes to the boil. Use a whisk if there are any lumps.

MAKES 1 CUP

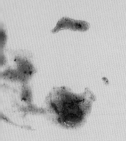

GRAVY

2 heaped tsp gravy powder
½ chicken or beef stock cube
or 1 heaped tsp stock powder
1 cup water
cooked meat juices (if available)
lemon juice (if needed)

1. In a saucepan, mix the gravy powder, stock cube or powder and ½ cup water, ensuring there are no lumps.
2. Add the remaining water and heat over a moderate heat, stirring continuously until the gravy thickens and comes to the boil.
3. When you have finished cooking your meat, pour the meat juices into the gravy for extra flavour.
4. If it is a bit too oily, carefully pour off the excess oil. Alternatively, add a squirt of lemon juice to the gravy to reduce the oiliness. If too thick, add more water.

SERVES 2

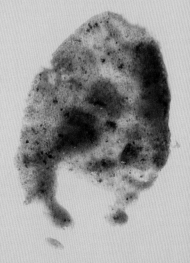

HOLLANDAISE SAUCE

This is a key ingredient in Eggs Benedict.

2 egg yolks
1 tsp white vinegar
2 tsp lemon juice
125 g butter, cubed

1. Half-fill a small saucepan with water and bring to the boil. Turn down the heat to very low and fit a heat-resistant bowl over it.
2. Add the egg yolks, vinegar, lemon juice and 1 small cube of butter to the bowl. Using a hand whisk, beat the mixture until the egg yolks thicken and become creamy. If it starts to get lumpy like scrambled eggs, take the bowl off the heat and continue with the next step.
3. Gradually add the rest of the butter, a cube at a time, beating each cube into the mixture before adding the next. (Return to the heat if necessary.)
4. Continue until the sauce is thick and creamy. Serve at room temperature with fish or vegetables.

MAKES ABOUT ¾ CUP

 Use boiled water from the kettle to save energy.

TIP If the sauce separates or 'curdles' due to overheating, make a quick recovery by adding an ice cube. This will restore the sauce to its former creamy glory.

Variation

QUICK BÉARNAISE SAUCE: Make a Hollandaise as above and add 1 Tbsp dried tarragon. Serve with steak.

BASIC WHITE SAUCE

30 g butter
2 Tbsp cake flour
1 cup milk
salt and pepper to taste

1. Melt the butter slowly in a saucepan over a moderate heat. Mix in the flour and heat gently for 1 minute, stirring occasionally (we call this a roux).
2. Remove the pan from the heat and whisk in a little of the milk, ensuring that there are no lumps.
3. Add the rest of the milk gradually, stirring all the time, and then return the pan to the heat. Keep stirring until the sauce thickens and comes to the boil. Use a whisk if there are any lumps. Season to taste.

MAKES 1 CUP

TIP Make a large batch of this sauce in one go and freeze it by the cupful in Ziploc™ bags or containers. Simply defrost as needed.

Variations

When making sauces, always taste them first before you add them to your dish.
Use the basic white sauce recipe above to make the following:

ANCHOVY SAUCE: add 1 tsp anchovy paste and serve with fish.
CHEESE SAUCE: add a handful of grated Cheddar cheese to the hot white sauce, stirring until the cheese melts. This will thicken the sauce further, so you may want to add more milk if it's too thick.
CHEESE AND WINE SAUCE: add ½ cup grated cheese and 1 Tbsp white wine to the hot white sauce and serve with fish or chicken.
MUSHROOM SAUCE: add 1 Tbsp soy sauce and 1 cup stir-fried sliced mushrooms and serve with steak, fish or chicken.
MUSTARD SAUCE: add 1 Tbsp wholegrain mustard and serve with chicken, pork or beef.
PARSLEY SAUCE: add a handful of chopped fresh parsley and serve with fish.
PINK SAUCE: add a squirt of tomato sauce to get the required taste and serve with fish.

FLAVOURED MAYONNAISE

Flavoured mayonnaise is useful for sandwiches, wraps, dips and adding to meat or fish.

Add any of the following to 1 cup French-style plain (not tangy) mayonnaise (or ½ cup mayonnaise and ½ cup plain yoghurt for a milder base):

Chillinaise: 1½ Tbsp tomato sauce and 1 tsp chilli sauce

Coriander mayonnaise: a good handful of destalked and shredded fresh coriander leaves

Garlic mayonnaise: 3–4 cloves garlic, peeled and finely chopped (This is great with plain meat or fish, potato wedges, baked potatoes or as a dip.)

Lemonnaise: juice of half a lemon

Mustanaise: 2 Tbsp wholegrain mustard

Pestonaise: ½ cup pesto

Sweet chillinaise: 2 Tbsp sweet chilli sauce

Tartare sauce: 1 Tbsp chopped chives, 1 tsp chopped capers, 1 Tbsp chopped gherkins and 1 Tbsp chopped fresh parsley (This makes a good dip and is excellent with crumbed calamari and potato wedges.)

Wasabi mayonnaise: a dash of wasabi

Tartare sauce

SOUP IT UP

CUCUMBER SOUP

This is a fairly chunky, cool, refreshing, green soup.

1 chicken or vegetable stock cube or	1 cup plain yoghurt
1 Tbsp stock powder	1 mint leaf, chopped
1 Tbsp boiling water	1 tsp garlic and herb seasoning
1 cup cold water	salt and pepper to taste
1 large cucumber, washed and diced	extra mint leaves for garnishing

1. Dissolve the stock cube or powder in the boiling water and then top up with the cold water.
2. Blitz everything in a blender and chill in the fridge. Garnish with fresh mint leaves and serve.

SERVES 2–3

AVOCADO SOUP

2 large ripe avocados, peeled and stoned	2 cups water
½ tsp grated onion	1 chicken or vegetable stock cube (crumbled) or
¼ cup plain yoghurt	1 Tbsp stock powder
a squirt of lemon juice	salt and pepper to taste
100 ml (½ can) tomato cocktail	a dash of Tabasco (optional)

1. Blitz everything in a blender and chill in the fridge.
2. Serve cold with French bread.

SERVES 2–3

LEEK AND POTATO SOUP

This is also known as Vichyssoise.

3 large leeks, white part only
1 Tbsp butter
1 large potato, peeled and diced
3 cups water
1 chicken or vegetable stock cube or 2 Tbsp stock powder
salt and pepper to taste
¼ cup cream
a handful of fresh chives, snipped

1. Trim, wash and slice the leeks.
2. Heat the butter in a medium saucepan over a low heat and add the leeks and potato. Cover and steam the vegetables for 2–3 minutes, stirring occasionally.
3. Add the water and stock cube or powder, and bring to the boil. Reduce the heat, cover and simmer over a low heat for 30 minutes. Stir occasionally to prevent sticking.
4. Remove from the heat and blitz in a blender, adding salt and pepper to taste. Chill in the fridge for at least 1 hour.
5. When ready to serve, mix in the cream and top each bowl with snipped chives.

SERVES 2–3

BROCCOLI SOUP

1 Tbsp oil	1 vegetable stock cube or 2 Tbsp stock powder
1 small onion, peeled and chopped	¼ cup grated Cheddar cheese
350 g broccoli florets, washed	salt and pepper to taste
3 cups water	a dash of cream (optional)

1. Heat the oil in a large saucepan over a low heat and cook the onion for 3 minutes, stirring occasionally.
2. Add the broccoli, water and stock cube or powder. Bring to the boil, put on the lid at an angle, then reduce the heat and simmer for 25 minutes.
3. Transfer to a blender with the cheese and liquidise until smooth.
4. Reheat before serving. Season to taste and add a dash of cream if desired.

SERVES 2–3

COURGETTE SOUP

1 Tbsp oil	1 chicken or vegetable stock cube or 1 heaped
1 small onion, peeled and chopped	Tbsp stock powder
450 g courgettes (baby marrows), washed	3 small mint leaves
and sliced	¼ cup plain yoghurt (optional)
2½ cups water	salt and pepper to taste

1. Heat the oil in a large saucepan over a low heat. Add the onion and courgettes, cover and cook for 5 minutes, stirring occasionally. Add the water, stock cube or powder and mint leaves.
2. Bring to the boil, then reduce the heat, cover and simmer for 25 minutes.
3. Transfer to a blender and liquidise until smooth.
4. Reheat before serving (or serve cold), then add the yoghurt (if using) and season to taste.

SERVES 2–3

THAI-STYLE BUTTERNUT SOUP

The amounts given in brackets are to help you double the recipe. Trust me, it's so good you'll want to!

500 g butternut, peeled and cubed (1 kg)

2 Tbsp oil (2 Tbsp)

a pinch of salt (a pinch)

1 small onion, peeled and finely chopped (1 medium)

1 Tbsp Thai red curry paste (2–3 Tbsp)

1½ cups water (4–5 cups)

1 chicken or vegetable stock cube or 1 Tbsp stock powder (3 cubes or 2 Tbsp powder)

1 cup coconut milk (1 x 400 ml can)

a handful of fresh coriander (optional)

1. Preheat the oven to 180 °C.
2. Put the butternut in a shallow roasting pan and drizzle over half of the oil. Sprinkle with the salt, cover with foil and cook for 30–40 minutes until soft.
3. Gently heat the remaining oil in a frying pan and fry the onion for 3–4 minutes.
4. Add the curry paste and fry for 1–2 minutes until fragrant.
5. Put the cooked butternut and onion in a food processor and add the water, stock cube or powder and coconut milk. Purée to as chunky or smooth as you like.
6. Reheat before serving and garnish with sprigs of fresh coriander if desired.

SERVES 2–3 (6–8)

CHICKEN NOODLE SOUP

This soup is even more wholesome if you use real, homemade chicken stock (see page 43).

4 cups boiling water

2 chicken stock cubes or
   2½ Tbsp chicken stock powder

1 chicken breast fillet, cut into thin strips

½ cup small pasta noodles or
   broken-up angel-hair pasta

½ cup cooked sweetcorn (canned will do)

1 spring onion, trimmed and chopped

½ cup frozen peas

1. Pour the water into a large saucepan and mix in the stock cubes or powder. Alternatively, use 4 cups homemade chicken stock.

2. Add the chicken and bring to the boil. Then reduce the heat and simmer for 5 minutes.

3. Stir in the pasta, sweetcorn and spring onion, turn up the heat and boil for about 12 minutes, until the pasta is soft.

4. Reduce the heat, add the peas and simmer for a further 2 minutes.

 Use boiled water from the kettle.

SERVES 2–3

TOMATO SOUP

This is so quick and easy, and it tastes as if you have gone to the trouble of roasting fresh tomatoes.

1 Tbsp oil
1 clove garlic, peeled and
finely chopped
1 x 410 g can tomato purée
2 cups water
1 chicken or vegetable stock cube or
2 heaped tsp stock powder
½ tsp sugar
⅓ cup cream
freshly ground black pepper to taste

1. Heat the oil in a large saucepan and gently fry the garlic for 1 minute.
2. Add the tomato purée, water, stock cube or powder and sugar. Simmer gently for 10 minutes.
3. Add the cream, heat through and serve with a generous sprinkling of black pepper.

SERVES 2–3

CARBO-LOADING

COOKING PASTA

Most pasta packets are 500 g, ideal for about 6 people. For 2–3 people, use about one third of a packet.

1. Bring a large saucepan of water to the boil over a high heat.
2. Add a drop of oil and a pinch of salt to make the water boil faster.
3. Add the pasta, breaking spaghetti in half, and stir once to separate.
4. Cook at a rapid boil for 10–12 minutes, until the pasta is just turning soft. This is called 'al dente', meaning slightly chewy, not soggy. To stop the water boiling over, put a cork or wooden spoon into the water. Drain and serve immediately with a sauce. It's best to make the sauce first or while the pasta is cooking.

Use boiled water from the kettle to save energy.

TIPS - If your pasta is cooked in advance, rinse it with cold water to stop it cooking further. Then reheat just before serving – pour boiling water over it and drain immediately.
- To prevent cooked pasta sticking together in a soggy mass, mix in a little oil or butter.

Tomato and chorizo pasta sauce

205 g (½ can) tomato purée	**2 tsp basil pesto**
¾ cup water	**1 cup thinly sliced chorizo or peeled mini salami**
½ chicken stock cube or 2 tsp stock powder	**½ cup cream**

1. Bring the tomato purée and water to the boil in a small saucepan over a moderate heat.
2. Add the chicken stock cube or powder, pesto and chorizo or salami.
3. Reduce the heat, cover and simmer gently for 10 minutes. Add the cream and heat through.
4. Mix the sauce into cooked pasta (see above) and serve.

SERVES 2–3

Napolitana (tomato and basil) sauce

1 Tbsp oil

1–2 cloves garlic, peeled and finely chopped

1 x 400 g can Italian tomatoes

2 tsp finely chopped fresh basil

1 tsp dried mixed herbs

¼ tsp sugar

1 tsp balsamic vinegar

salt and pepper to taste

½ cup grated cheese to serve

1. Heat the oil in a medium saucepan and cook the garlic over a moderate heat for 1 minute.
2. Add the tomatoes and their juices, and mash with a fork.
3. Mix in the basil, herbs, sugar and vinegar, and bring to the boil.
4. Reduce the heat and simmer for 15 minutes. Season to taste.
5. Pour over cooked pasta (see page 57) and serve topped with the grated cheese.

SERVES 2–3

Alfredo (ham, cream and mushroom) sauce

30 g butter
1 clove garlic, peeled and finely chopped
250 g button mushrooms, wiped and sliced
½ cup grated Cheddar cheese
1 cup cream
4 large slices ham, cut into strips
salt and freshly ground black pepper to taste
grated Parmesan cheese to serve (optional)

1. Melt the butter in a medium frying pan over a moderate heat.
2. Add the garlic and mushrooms, and fry for 5 minutes.
3. Mix the Cheddar cheese into the cream and add to the pan. Stir continuously while the sauce thickens.
4. Mix in the ham and heat through. Season to taste.
5. Pour over cooked pasta (see page 57) and serve with Parmesan cheese if desired.

SERVES 2–3

The Italians are quite strict about which sauces go with which types of pasta. As a general and simple rule, thin sauces go with thin pastas and thick sauces go with more chunky pastas. Pasta shapes hold the sauce well. Fish/seafood is better with spaghetti or linguine, whereas bolognaise seems to go with anything. The choice is yours.

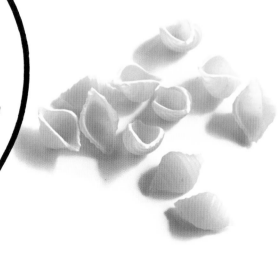

CHICKEN, BROCCOLI
and pesto pasta

This is a delicious meal in one dish. Pesto is usually made with toasted pine nuts, but as these are fairly scarce and expensive, cashews make a very good substitute. Store pesto in a sealed jar in the fridge for up to a week.

½ head broccoli, roughly divided into florets

¼ cup flaked almonds

1 Tbsp oil

1 small clove garlic, peeled and chopped

2 large chicken breast fillets, sliced into thin strips

1½ Tbsp soy sauce

1 cup cream

a squirt of lemon juice

1 Tbsp basil pesto

freshly ground black pepper to taste

BASIL PESTO (MAKES 350 ML)

1 large clove garlic, peeled and
   roughly chopped

60 g fresh basil leaves, washed

1 cup canola oil

½ cup roasted salted cashew nuts

½ cup grated Parmesan cheese

salt and pepper to taste

1. Cook the broccoli in a pot of boiling water for 5–7 minutes. Drain and keep warm in the pot.
2. Toast the almonds (without oil) in a large frying pan over a low heat for 5 minutes, shaking the pan now and then to toast them evenly. Set aside in a small dish.
3. Heat the oil in the frying pan over a moderate heat and stir-fry the garlic and chicken strips for 7 minutes, until the chicken is lightly brown all over.
4. Turn down the heat and stir in the soy sauce, cream and lemon juice.
5. Bring to the boil, then reduce the heat and simmer very gently for 8–10 minutes to thicken slightly. Start cooking your pasta in the meantime (see page 57).
6. To make the pesto, blitz the garlic, basil and half of the oil in a blender. Add the cashews and cheese with the rest of the oil and blitz further. Season to taste.
7. Stir 1 Tbsp of the pesto and some black pepper into the sauce.
8. Place the cooked pasta into a serving dish and pour over the chicken and sauce. Add the broccoli and mix in by gently turning the pasta. Sprinkle the toasted almonds on top and serve.

SERVES 2

RATATOUILLE PASTA BAKE

Penne or macaroni is good for this.

1 quantity of ratatouille (see page 156)
1 cup grated mozzarella or Cheddar cheese

1. Start making the ratatouille as described on page 156.
2. Cook your pasta (see page 57).
3. Switch on the oven's grill.
4. Mix the ratatouille into the cooked pasta and transfer the mixture to an ovenproof dish.
5. Top with the grated cheese and place under the grill (not too close) for 5 minutes, until it is bubbling and the cheese has melted. Serve immediately.

SERVES 2–3

MACARONI CHEESE

Use macaroni for this recipe.

1 cup cheese sauce (see page 46), warmed
½ cup grated Cheddar cheese

1. Cook the macaroni (see page 57).
2. Switch on the oven's grill.
3. Place the cooked, drained macaroni into an ovenproof dish and pour over the warmed cheese sauce. Mix well.
4. Top with the grated cheese and place under the grill for a few minutes, until the sauce is bubbling and the cheese is golden brown. Serve immediately.

SERVES 2–3

BEEF LASAGNE

2 cups bolognaise sauce (see page 66)
3 cups cheese sauce (see page 46)
4–6 sheets dry ('precooked') lasagne
½–1 cup grated cheese

1. Preheat the oven to 180 °C.
2. Spread half of the bolognaise sauce over the base of a roughly 22 x 16 cm rectangular ovenproof dish or baking tin.
3. Cover with 1 cup cheese sauce, then a single layer of 2–3 lasagne sheets, overlapping to fit the dish.
4. Repeat with another layer of the remaining bolognaise sauce, another 1 cup cheese sauce and the remaining lasagne sheets.
5. Pour over the remaining cup of cheese sauce and sprinkle the grated cheese on top.
6. Bake for 40–45 minutes until the pasta is soft and the cheese is bubbling and golden brown.

SERVES 2

SPAGHETTI BOLOGNAISE

Use spaghetti for this recipe (see page 57).

1 Tbsp oil
1 onion, peeled and chopped
1 clove garlic, peeled and finely chopped
250 g beef mince
1 x 400 g can Italian tomatoes
1 tsp dried mixed herbs
2 Tbsp tomato purée
½ beef stock cube or 1 tsp stock powder
grated Parmesan or Cheddar cheese to serve

1. Heat the oil in a medium saucepan and fry the onion and garlic over a moderate heat for 3–4 minutes, stirring occasionally.
2. Add the mince and keep stirring to brown the meat all over. Chop it with the spoon into crumbly bits.
3. Mash in the tomatoes and add the herbs, tomato purée and stock cube or powder. Mix well and bring to the boil. Then reduce the heat, cover and simmer for 30 minutes, stirring occasionally. Add a little water if necessary.
4. Spoon the bolognaise over the cooked spaghetti and serve with grated cheese.

SERVES 2

TUNA BAKE

Use macaroni for this recipe (see page 57).

1 x 170 g can tuna, drained
1 cup cheese sauce (see page 46), warmed
a little milk if necessary
½ cup grated Cheddar cheese

1. While the pasta is cooking, mash the tuna in a saucepan and add the cheese sauce. Mix well and heat gently over a low heat. Add a little more milk if the sauce is too thick.
2. Switch on the oven's grill.
3. Put the drained macaroni into an ovenproof dish and pour over the warmed tuna and cheese sauce. Mix well.
4. Top with the grated cheese and place under the grill for a few minutes until bubbling and golden brown. Serve immediately.

SERVES 2–3

Be sure to buy only dolphin-friendly tuna. It will tell you on the label.

PASTA WITH MUSSELS IN TOMATO AND HERBS

Mussels are cheap and make an excellent pasta sauce with fettuccine or a starter served with French bread.

1 Tbsp oil
1 Tbsp butter
1 small onion, peeled and finely chopped
1–2 cloves garlic, peeled and finely chopped
1 x 400 g can Italian tomatoes
1½ tsp finely chopped fresh basil
1½ tsp finely chopped fresh coriander
salt and pepper to taste
300–400 g mussel 'meat' (no shells)
extra fresh coriander to garnish

1. Heat the oil and butter in a medium saucepan over a moderate heat and fry the onion and garlic for 3–4 minutes, stirring occasionally.
2. Mash in the tomatoes with their juice, add the herbs and bring to the boil.
3. Reduce the heat to very low, cover and simmer for 10 minutes. Remove the lid and simmer for a further 5 minutes to reduce slightly. Season to taste.
4. Add the mussels, heat through and serve immediately over cooked pasta (see page 57), garnished with fresh coriander.
5. If you want to add some frozen mussels in half shells, boil them for 10 minutes in a large pot of water. Add to the pasta before serving.

SERVES 2–3

COOKING RICE

Rice is very easy to cook perfectly, as long as you time it and don't let it overcook into a mushy mess. As rice expands to almost 3 times its volume in cooking, 1 cup of white rice serves 3–4 people.

Long-grain white rice

1 cup long-grain white rice
2 cups water
a pinch of salt

1. Rinse the rice in a sieve.
2. Put the water and salt in a saucepan and bring to the boil. Add the rice, mixing once to separate.
3. Cover and reduce the heat to very low, so that it is just bubbling. Cook for exactly 12 minutes. All the liquid should be absorbed. If it looks a bit starchy on top, rinse through in a sieve with boiling water. The rice is now ready to serve.

 Use boiled water from the kettle to save energy.

Basmati rice

This delicious rice has a slightly nutty aroma.

1 cup basmati rice
2 cups water
a pinch of salt

1. Rinse the rice well in a sieve until the water runs clear.
2. Put the rice in a saucepan and add the water and salt.
3. Cover and bring to the boil, then uncover and reduce the heat to low, so that it is just bubbling. Cook for 12 minutes exactly. All the liquid should be absorbed. The rice is now ready to serve.

Brown rice

This takes longer to cook and doesn't expand as much as white rice. One cup will serve 2–3 people.

2 cups water
a pinch of salt
1 cup brown rice

1. Put the water and salt in a saucepan and bring to the boil. Add the rice, mixing once to separate.
2. Cover and reduce the heat to very low, so that it is just bubbling. Cook for 25–30 minutes until the rice is tender. It is now ready to serve.

 Use boiling water from the kettle to save energy.

Flavoured rice

You can flavour rice to go with a meat or vegetable dish or simply serve it plain.

Here are a couple of ideas to vary the taste of rice:

- Add a stock cube to the boiling water in which the rice will be cooked, and add about 3 minutes to the cooking time.
- Fry a chopped small onion in a little oil and add to cooked rice.
- Add grated raw carrot and chopped parsley to cooked rice to serve with chicken or fish.
- Toast flaked almonds in a dry frying pan over a moderate heat and add to cooked rice.

TOMATO SAVOURY RICE

This goes well with grilled fish or meat.

1 Tbsp oil
1 Tbsp butter
1 small onion, peeled and finely chopped
½ medium red pepper, deseeded and finely chopped
1 cup uncooked white rice, rinsed
1 x 400 g can Italian tomatoes
1 Tbsp chicken or vegetable stock powder or 1 stock cube
½ cup water
salt and pepper to taste

1. Heat the oil and butter in a large frying pan over a moderate heat and fry the onion and red pepper for 5 minutes.
2. Stir in the rice to coat in the oil and butter. Add the tomatoes with their juice and break them up with a fork.
3. Add the stock powder or cube and water, and season to taste.
4. Bring to the boil, then reduce the heat to very low, cover the pan and simmer for 20–25 minutes, until the rice is tender and all the liquid has been absorbed.

SERVES 2–4

TIP For a vegetarian dish to serve 2 people, add fried mushrooms, courgettes, boiled peas and carrots.

EGG FRIED RICE

¾ cup uncooked white rice, rinsed
1½ cups water
1½ Tbsp oil
4 spring onions, sliced (including some of the green)
1 egg
a dash of soy sauce

1. Put the rice and water in a small saucepan, cover and bring to the boil. Turn down the heat to low, uncover and simmer for 12 minutes until the water is absorbed.
2. Heat 1 Tbsp of the oil in a large frying pan over a moderate heat. Add the rice and stir to coat. Add the spring onions and stir-fry for 3–4 minutes.
3. Make a hollow in the middle of the rice mixture and add the remaining oil to it. Break the egg into the oil and fry, without stirring, for 2–3 minutes.
4. Next, break up the egg with a spatula, and continue to stir-fry and mix into the rice for a further minute.
5. Remove from the heat, drizzle with soy sauce and serve immediately.

Variations

Add 2 tsp chicken or vegetable stock powder (or ½ stock cube) to the water when boiling the rice and cook for 15 minutes.
Add cooked vegetables, such as peas, diced carrots, sweetcorn or beans to the dish before serving.

SERVES 2

EGG FRIED RICE WITH SMOKED HADDOCK

This is a meal in one dish and can be stretched to serve 3 or 4 people if you use a full cup of uncooked rice and 500 g haddock (leave the other ingredients the same).

a portion of egg fried rice (see opposite)
1 extra egg
1 large carrot, peeled and grated
½ cup frozen peas, covered in boiling water for 2 minutes
300–400 g smoked haddock
1 cup milk
1 Tbsp butter
1 Tbsp cake flour

1. Make the egg fried rice as on the opposite page, but add an extra egg. Before removing from the heat, mix in the carrot and drained peas. Transfer to a serving dish and cover to keep warm.
2. Put the haddock in a single layer in a medium saucepan. Cover with the milk and bring to the boil over a moderate heat. Then reduce the heat and simmer for 8–10 minutes until the fish flakes easily. Remove the haddock from the pan, reserving the milk.
3. Flake the haddock in bite-sized chunks over the rice, mixing it in gently. Recover the dish to keep it warm.
4. Melt the butter in a small saucepan over a low heat and mix in the flour. Heat gently for 1 minute, stirring occasionally.
5. Remove the pan from the heat and gradually whisk in the reserved milk. The sauce will thicken immediately as the milk is hot, but the sauce should still be fairly thin.
6. Heat the sauce through once more before serving separately in a jug or bowl, alongside the rice and haddock.

SERVES 2

COOKING POTATOES

Boiled potatoes

Use 1 medium/large potato per person.

1. Peel, wash and cut the potatoes in half.
2. Boil for 15–20 minutes in a pot of water until soft, but still firm.
3. Drain and serve.

Mashed potatoes

Use 1 large potato per person.

1. Peel, wash and cut the potatoes into small cubes.
2. Boil for 20 minutes in a pot of water until soft.
3. Drain, add a thick slice of butter and a little milk and mash until smooth, but not sloppy. Season with salt and pepper.
4. For a richer version, add 2 Tbsp smooth cream cheese.

TIP Instead of peeling the potatoes, microwave them unpeeled for 6–7 minutes per potato, then tear off the skin easily with your fingers. Put the peeled cooked potatoes in a bowl and mash as above.

Roast potatoes

Use 2 medium potatoes per person.

1. Preheat the oven to 180 °C.
2. Peel, wash and cut the potatoes in half lengthways.
3. Boil for 12 minutes in a pot of water.
4. Drain and put into a shallow baking dish (a baking tin is best as potatoes tend to take longer to cook in a glass or china dish) with ½ cup oil. Turn the potatoes in the oil to coat them and sprinkle with salt.
5. Bake for 1 hour, turning the potatoes once after 40 minutes. They should be brown and crispy on the outside.

Diced roast potatoes

Use 1½ large potatoes per person, as they tend to shrink in the roasting.

1. Preheat the oven to 180 °C.
2. Peel, wash and cut the potatoes in half.
3. Boil for 12 minutes in a pot of water, then drain.
4. Cut the par-cooked potatoes into fairly small cubes and place in a shallow baking dish (a baking tin is best as potatoes tend to take longer to cook in a glass or china dish) with enough oil to almost cover the base of the dish. Coat the potatoes in the oil and sprinkle with salt. Add a sprig of rosemary for extra flavour.
5. Bake for 45 minutes, turning once after 20 minutes. They should be brown and crispy all over.

Baked potatoes

Use 1 large potato per person.

1. Preheat the oven to 180 °C.
2. Wash the skin of the unpeeled potatoes and cut a cross in the top of each.
3. Bake for 90 minutes until soft inside and crispy on the outside.

 To save energy, microwave the potatoes first for 6 minutes per potato, to soften slightly, and then bake in the oven for 45 minutes to cook through and crisp up.

You can add various toppings to baked potatoes to make them a meal in themselves:

- Cut the cooked potatoes in half, mash some butter into each half with a fork and sprinkle with grated cheese. Place under the grill for 3 minutes.
- Fry diced bacon in a little oil until brown and crispy and scatter over the cheesy baked potatoes above.
- Squeeze the cooked potato open, keeping the cross shape on top, and top with sour cream, chopped chives and a generous pinch of freshly ground black pepper.
- Cut the cooked potatoes in half, add butter to melt in and top with garlic mayonnaise or cream cheese.
- Cut the cooked potatoes in half and top with savoury mince (see page 103) or bolognaise (see page 66).

POTATO BAKE

2 large potatoes, peeled, washed and finely sliced
salt and pepper to taste
1 cup cream
¾ cup grated cheese

1. Preheat the oven to 180 °C.
2. Layer the potato slices in a shallow baking dish. Season to taste and pour over the cream, ensuring that all the slices are covered.
3. Top with the grated cheese, cover with a lid or foil and bake for 40 minutes. Remove the lid or foil and bake for a further 20 minutes to brown on top.

SERVES 2

COOKING COUSCOUS

Couscous is good with meat or fish, or as a salad if you add tasty ingredients. A 250 g packet will be enough for 4–6 people. A cup of couscous serves 2–3.

1 cup couscous
¾ cup boiling water
1 Tbsp oil or butter

1. Place the couscous in a medium-sized bowl and pour over the boiling water.
2. Cover with clingfilm and leave to stand for 10 minutes, until all the water has been absorbed.
3. Remove the clingfilm, fluff up the couscous with a fork and mix in the oil or butter.

Add a dressing and/or topping for flavour. Here are a few suggestions – quantities are for 2 people:

- **Refreshing dressing**: Mix 1 tsp grated lemon rind, 1 Tbsp oil, chopped parsley, mint and coriander, salt and pepper. Serve with fish or chicken.
- **Spicy dressing**: Mix 1 tsp each of chopped garlic, chopped ginger and chopped chilli with 1 Tbsp oil. Serve with meat or fish.
- **Greek style**: Add chopped cucumber, halved baby tomatoes, pitted chopped olives and feta with a dressing of chopped garlic, herbs, 1 Tbsp lemon juice and 1 Tbsp oil.
- **Roast vegetables**: Roast a selection of vegetables and mix into the couscous (see page 155 for some help with the vegetables). Add a dressing of 1 Tbsp balsamic vinegar and 1 Tbsp oil. Serve with meat, fish or on its own.

BUTTERNUT AND FETA COUSCOUS SALAD

2 cups peeled and diced butternut
oil for drizzling
1 cup couscous
½ cup crumbled feta cheese
fresh coriander to garnish

DRESSING
1 Tbsp lemon juice
1 tsp cumin
1 Tbsp oil

1. Preheat the oven to 180 °C.
2. Place the butternut in a shallow roasting pan, drizzle with oil and roast for 30 minutes, turning once after 15 minutes.
3. In the meantime, cook the couscous as directed on page 81.
4. Mix the roasted butternut into the cooked couscous and add the feta.
5. Mix the dressing in a cup and pour over the couscous salad. Garnish with fresh coriander and serve.

SERVES 2

SPICY CHICKPEAS WITH COUSCOUS

1 Tbsp oil
1 large clove garlic, peeled and
   finely chopped
1 medium onion, peeled and chopped
½–1 tsp curry powder
1 x 400 g can Italian tomatoes
1 x 400 g can chickpeas, drained and rinsed
1 carrot, peeled and thinly sliced
a little plain yoghurt (optional)
1 cup couscous

1. Heat the oil in a medium saucepan and
   fry the garlic and onion over a moderate
   heat for 3–4 minutes.
2. Add the curry powder and fry for a further
   1 minute until fragrant.
3. Add the tomatoes, mashing them up
   a bit, and mix in the chickpeas and carrot.
   Cover and simmer on a low heat for
   15–20 minutes. If the sauce is too spicy, add
   a little plain yoghurt to cool it down. This
   gives a nice creamy texture as a variation.
4. Meanwhile, cook the couscous as directed
   on page 81.
5. Stir the chickpea sauce into the cooked
   couscous and serve.

SERVES 2

HALLOUMI AND CHORIZO COUSCOUS SALAD

1 cup couscous
1 Tbsp oil
4–6 fingers halloumi
½ cup sliced chorizo
¼ cup diced red pepper
¼ cup finely chopped onion

DRESSING
1 Tbsp lemon juice
1 Tbsp oil
salt and pepper to taste

1. Cook the couscous as directed on page 81.
2. Heat the oil in a medium frying pan over a moderate heat and fry the halloumi, chorizo, red pepper and onion, turning and stirring for 5 minutes until brown and crispy at the edges.
3. Chop up the halloumi and mix all of the fried ingredients into the cooked couscous.
4. Mix the dressing in a cup and pour over the couscous salad.

SERVES 2

BREADS
BANANA BREAD

2 cups cake flour
2 tsp baking powder
½ tsp bicarbonate of soda
½ tsp ground cinnamon (optional)
2 eggs
90 g butter
¼ cup honey
3 large ripe bananas, peeled and sliced
a squirt of lemon juice

1. Preheat the oven to 180 °C.
2. Lightly grease a small loaf tin (about 20 x 9 cm) with oil and dust with ½ tsp flour.
3. Blend all of the ingredients in a food processor or beat well in a mixing bowl until smooth.
4. Pour into the loaf tin and bake for 40 minutes. Test if it's ready by inserting a skewer or toothpick in the middle. If it comes out clean, the bread is done.
5. Allow to cool for 10 minutes before slicing and serving warm with butter.

Variation
Mix in ½ cup chopped walnuts or pecan nuts before baking.

MAKES 1 SMALL LOAF

CHEESE BREAD

This is delicious straight from the oven. It's probably a good idea to make double, so there's enough to share. Just use a slightly longer loaf tin.

2 cups self-raising flour
1 cup buttermilk
1 cup grated Cheddar cheese
3 Tbsp thick white onion
    soup powder

1. Preheat the oven to 180 °C.
2. Lightly grease a small loaf tin (about 20 x 9 cm) with oil and dust with ½ tsp flour.
3. Mix all of the ingredients into a dough and place in the loaf tin.
4. Bake for 50 minutes until golden brown. Test if it's ready by inserting a skewer or toothpick in the middle. If it comes out clean, the bread is done.

MAKES 1 SMALL LOAF

GARLIC BREAD

1 short French loaf (about 40 cm long) **3 sprigs of fresh parsley, chopped**
2 tsp finely chopped garlic **60 g butter, softened**

1. Preheat the oven to 200 °C.
2. Mash the garlic and parsley into the butter with a fork.
3. Cut diagonal slits in the French loaf at about 2 cm intervals, leaving the bottom crust whole, and spread the garlic butter generously into the slits. Wrap the bread in foil with the opening at the top. Fold the ends over at the top and sides so that the bread is fully enclosed.
4. Bake for 20 minutes until the butter has melted.

TIP Adding parsley reduces the odour of garlic!

ANCHOVY BREAD

Serve this with fish or as a snack.

1 short French loaf (about 40 cm long) **60 g butter, softened**
3 rounded tsp anchovy paste

1. Preheat the oven to 200 °C.
2. Mix the anchovy paste into the butter.
3. Cut diagonal slits in the French loaf at about 2 cm intervals, leaving the bottom crust whole, and spread the anchovy butter generously into the slits. Wrap the bread in foil with the opening at the top. Fold the ends over at the top and sides so that the bread is fully enclosed.
4. Bake for 20 minutes until the butter has melted.

CHICKEN

THAI COCONUT CHICKEN

This is a quick favourite that only takes about 15 minutes to make.

1 x 400 ml can coconut cream
2 large chicken breast fillets, rinsed and cut into strips
2 spring onions, thinly sliced, including a little of the dark green bit
½ tsp deseeded and finely chopped red chilli
1 Tbsp fish sauce
1½ Tbsp freshly squeezed lime or lemon juice
a handful of fresh coriander, washed and destalked (not chopped)

1. Heat the coconut cream in a medium saucepan over a moderate heat. As soon as it starts to boil, reduce the heat and add the chicken. Simmer very gently, so the liquid gives an occasional bubble, for 5 minutes.
2. Add the spring onion and chilli, and cook for a further 2 minutes.
3. Remove from the heat and stir in the fish sauce, lime or lemon juice and most of the coriander.
4. Garnish with the remaining coriander and serve with rice or noodles.

SERVES 2

THAI RED CHICKEN CURRY

2 large chicken breast fillets
4 tsp Thai red curry paste (for moderate heat)
½ x 400 ml can coconut milk
a handful of fresh coriander (optional)

1. Preheat the oven to 180 °C.
2. Rinse the chicken fillets and place them in an ovenproof dish.
3. Spread the curry paste over the chicken and pour over the coconut milk. With the back of a spoon, roughly mix the curry paste into the coconut milk.
4. Bake for 30 minutes.
5. Garnish with fresh coriander, if desired, and serve with rice or noodles.

SERVES 2

> Always make sure that your chicken is fresh. If it smells bad, throw it away, as the bacteria will give you food poisoning.

CHICKEN IN MUSHROOM SAUCE

1 Tbsp oil
4–6 chicken thighs, skin and fat removed
1 Tbsp butter
1 clove garlic, peeled and finely chopped
1 small onion, peeled and finely chopped
1 x 250 g punnet large brown mushrooms, chopped
2 level tsp cornflour
2 Tbsp soy sauce
½ cup cream
1 cup chicken stock made with 1 cup water and ½ stock
 cube or 2 tsp stock powder
freshly ground black pepper to taste

1. Preheat the oven to 180 °C.
2. Heat the oil in a large frying pan over a moderate heat and brown the chicken for 5 minutes on each side, then place in a single layer in an ovenproof dish.
3. Melt the butter in the same pan and gently fry the garlic, onion and mushrooms for 3 minutes, scraping in the dried pan juices and stirring occasionally. Remove from the heat.
4. In a cup, mix the cornflour with the soy sauce until smooth. Mix in the cream and then pour over the onion and mushroom mix, stirring it in.
5. Add the stock, return the pan to the heat and keep stirring until the sauce thickens. Season with black pepper to taste.
6. Pour the mushroom sauce over the chicken pieces and bake for 40 minutes.
7. Serve with pasta or rice and vegetables.

SERVES 2

STIR-FRIED CHICKEN WITH NUTS

1 heaped tsp cornflour

1 Tbsp soy sauce

2 large chicken breast fillets, washed and thinly sliced

2 Tbsp almonds or cashew nuts

1 Tbsp sesame or cooking oil

1 clove garlic, peeled and finely chopped

2 tsp oyster sauce (optional)

1. Mix the cornflour and soy sauce in a large bowl. Add the chicken strips, mix well and allow to marinade for a few minutes.
2. Meanwhile, toast the nuts (without oil) over a moderate heat in a wok or large frying pan, shaking them to toast evenly. Remove the nuts from the pan and set aside.
3. Heat the oil in the same pan and stir-fry the garlic and marinated chicken for 5–7 minutes. The cornflour will thicken, coating the chicken in a delicious brown crust.
4. Stir in the oyster sauce, if using, and the toasted nuts, and then remove from the heat.
5. Serve with rice or noodles.

Variation

Stir-fry a selection of vegetables, such as baby corn, shredded cabbage, carrots cut into matchsticks, shredded spinach, sliced mushrooms and bean sprouts, in a little oil and mix into the chicken dish.

SERVES 2

Ensure that any leftover cooked chicken is kept cold in the fridge, and only reheat once more. Use leftover chicken to make soup, pies, toasted sandwiches and a variety of other dishes.

IN PEANUT CHILLI SAUCE

This makes a subtle and tasty sauce that can be stretched to serve 4 people if you double the chicken and add only an extra ½ cup chicken stock. All the other ingredients remain the same.

½ cup coconut milk
1 heaped Tbsp peanut butter
½ tsp finely chopped red chilli
1 Tbsp chicken stock powder or 1 stock cube
½ cup water
1 Tbsp oil
1 small onion, peeled and chopped
1 clove garlic, peeled and finely chopped
2 large chicken breast fillets, washed and cubed
salt and pepper to taste

1. Mix the coconut milk, peanut butter, chilli, stock powder or cube and water in a bowl until smooth.
2. Heat the oil in a large frying pan over a moderate heat and fry the onion and garlic for 4 minutes until soft.
3. Add the chicken and stir-fry for 5 minutes to lightly brown all over.
4. Stir in the peanut chilli sauce and bring to the boil. Reduce the heat to low and simmer for 5 minutes.
5. Season to taste and serve with rice or noodles.

SERVES 2

ITALIAN CHICKEN

The amounts given in brackets are to help you double the recipe.

2 large chicken breast fillets, rinsed (4)
1 Tbsp oil (1 Tbsp)
1 Tbsp butter (1 Tbsp)
1 clove garlic, peeled and finely chopped (2 cloves)
½ small onion, peeled and finely chopped (1 small)
125 g button mushrooms, rinsed and sliced (250 g)
½ tsp garlic and herb seasoning (½ tsp)
½ cup tomato purée (¾ cup)
½ cup strong chicken stock made with ½ cup water and 1 Tbsp stock powder or 1 stock cube (½ cup)
2 tsp basil pesto or chopped fresh basil (3 tsp)
salt and pepper to taste
¾ cup grated cheese (1 cup)

1. Preheat the oven to 180 °C.
2. Place the chicken fillets in an ovenproof dish.
3. Heat the oil and butter in a large frying pan over a moderate heat and gently stir-fry the garlic, onion, mushrooms and garlic and herb seasoning for 5 minutes. Pour this over the chicken.
4. Mix the tomato purée, stock, pesto or basil, salt and pepper in a bowl and pour over the chicken.
5. Sprinkle the cheese on top, cover with foil and bake for 20 minutes. Remove the foil and bake for a further 20 minutes.

TIP If the baking dish is full, put the dish on a baking tray to catch any spills – it will save you cleaning the oven!

SERVES 2 (4)

CHICKEN PIE

The amounts given in brackets are to help you double the recipe.

2 cooked chicken breast fillets (1 whole cooked chicken)
½ cup cooked sweetcorn or drained canned corn (1 cup)
1 cup stock sauce* (see page 43) (3 cups)
2 tsp soy sauce (1½ Tbsp)
½ x 400 g pkt ready-made puff pastry, thawed at room temperature (1 pkt)
1 Tbsp milk (1 Tbsp)

1. Preheat the oven to 200 °C.
2. If using uncooked chicken fillets, simmer the fillets in 2 cups stock for 20 minutes, and then remove, reserving the stock to make the stock sauce (see page 43). Slice the chicken and put in a small pie dish.
3. If using a whole cooked chicken, remove the skin and cut the chicken off the bone. Chop the meat into bite-size chunks and put in a large pie dish.
4. In a medium saucepan, mix the sweetcorn with the stock sauce and stir in the soy sauce. Heat through, then pour the warmed sauce over the chicken and mix in gently.
5. Roll out the pastry to just bigger than the pie dish. Dab the outside edge of the dish with milk and cover with the pastry, gluing it down on the milky edges.
6. Brush the top of the pie with a little more milk and bake in the oven for 25–30 minutes, until the pastry is puffed and golden brown.

* You can use canned cream of chicken or mushroom soup instead, which is easier, but not as tasty.

TIP To stop the pie sinking in the middle, put an upside-down glass or ovenproof eggcup in the middle of the dish to support the pastry during baking.

SERVES 2 (4–6)

ROAST CHICKEN with
GRAVY, ROAST POTATOES AND VEGETABLES

1 whole chicken, no giblets
1 clove garlic, peeled
and squashed
½ lemon
dried origanum
½ cup water

ROAST VEGETABLES
a selection of vegetables,
chopped and/or sliced
oil for drizzling
garlic and herb salt
for sprinkling

ROAST POTATOES
1–2 medium potatoes
per person
½ cup oil
salt for sprinkling

GRAVY
3–4 heaped tsp
gravy powder
½ chicken stock cube or
1 tsp stock powder
1 cup hot water
cooked meat juices

Chicken

1. Preheat oven to 180 °C.
2. Cut a piece of tin foil big enough to wrap the chicken. Lay the foil flat (shiny side down) in a roasting pan.
3. Rinse the chicken inside and out and place it, breast side up, in the middle of the foil.
4. Put the whole garlic clove inside the chicken cavity, squeeze the lemon over the top and put the lemon skin inside the cavity too. Sprinkle over the origanum.
5. Bring up the edges of the foil and pour the water around the chicken. Fold the foil over at the top and seal the sides so that the chicken is totally enclosed.
6. Cook in the centre of the oven for 30 minutes per 500 g weight. A large (1.5 kg) chicken, enough for 4 people, will take about 90 minutes.
7. After 45 minutes, remove the chicken from the oven and open the foil. Return to the oven for the remaining time for the chicken to cook through and brown.
8. As soon as the chicken goes into the oven, start on the roast vegetables and potatoes.

Roast vegetables

1. Place the vegetables in a single layer in a baking tin, drizzle oil over them and add a sprinkling of garlic and herb salt.
2. Bake in the oven with the chicken for about 40 minutes, turning once after 20 minutes.

Roast potatoes

1. Peel, wash and cut the potatoes in half lengthways. Boil for 12 minutes in a pot of water, then drain and put in a shallow baking tin with the oil. Turn the potatoes in the oil to coat them and sprinkle with salt.
2. Bake in the oven with the chicken for 1 hour, turning the potatoes after 30 minutes. They should be brown and crispy on the outside.

Gravy

1. Just before the chicken is ready, start making the gravy. In a saucepan, mix the gravy powder, stock cube or powder and ½ cup hot water into a smooth paste.
2. Add the remaining hot water and heat over a moderate heat, stirring continuously until the sauce thickens and comes to the boil.
3. When you have finished cooking the chicken, pour the meat juices from the foil into the gravy for extra flavour. If the gravy is a bit too oily, carefully pour off the excess oil.

To carve the chicken, slice off the legs and wings, then thinly slice the breast, downwards, onto the plate. There are also nice bits underneath, which you can dig out with a knife or your fingers. Serve with the roast potatoes, vegetables and gravy.

 Turn the oven off 5–10 minutes before the roasting time is complete, keeping the door shut.

SERVES 4–6

MINCE AND MACARONI BAKE

The amounts given in brackets are to help you double the recipe.

¼ x 500 g pkt macaroni (½ x 500 g pkt)

1 Tbsp oil (1 Tbsp)

1 small onion, peeled and finely chopped (1 medium)

1 clove garlic, peeled and finely chopped (2 cloves)

250 g lean beef mince (500 g)

½ x 400 g can Italian tomatoes (1 x 400 g can)

2½ Tbsp tomato purée (½ cup)

1 Tbsp basil pesto or 1 tsp chopped fresh basil (2–3 Tbsp pesto or 2 tsp fresh)

salt and pepper to taste

1 egg yolk (still 1)

1 cup cheese sauce (see page 46) (2 cups)

½ cup grated cheese (1 cup)

1. Preheat the oven to 180 °C. Grease an ovenproof dish with a little oil.
2. Bring a large saucepan of water to the boil over a high heat. Add a drop of oil and a pinch of salt, and add the macaroni, stirring once to separate. Cook at a rapid boil for 10–12 minutes, then drain and put the macaroni in the greased dish.
3. Heat the oil in a medium saucepan and fry the onion and garlic over a moderate heat for 3–4 minutes.
4. Add the mince and cook for about 5 minutes, stirring continuously, until browned all over. Chop it with the spoon into crumbly bits.
5. Mash the tomatoes into the mince with a fork, and then mix in the tomato purée and pesto or fresh basil.
6. Cover and simmer over a low heat for 20 minutes, stirring occasionally. Season to taste.
7. Pour the mince mixture over the macaroni and mix well.
8. In a small bowl, mix the egg yolk with the cheese sauce. Spread this evenly over the macaroni and mince, and sprinkle the grated cheese on top.
9. Bake for 20 minutes until bubbling and golden on top.

 Use boiled water from the kettle to save energy.

SERVES 2–3 (6)

CHILLI CON CARNE

The amounts given in brackets are to help you double the recipe.

1 Tbsp oil (1 Tbsp)
1 small onion, peeled and chopped (1 large)
1 clove garlic, peeled and chopped (2 cloves)
250 g lean beef mince (500 g)
1 Tbsp beef stock powder or 1 stock cube (2 Tbsp or 2 cubes)
½ tsp dried mixed herbs (1 tsp)
1–2 tsp finely chopped chilli (3–4 tsp)
½ x 410 g can chopped peeled tomatoes (1 x 410 g can)
1 x 200 ml can tomato cocktail (still 1 x 200 ml can)
½ x 410 g can red kidney beans, drained (1 x 410 g can)
salt and pepper to taste

1. Heat the oil in a medium saucepan and fry the onion and garlic over a moderate heat for 5 minutes.
2. Add the mince and cook for 7–10 minutes, stirring continuously, until browned all over. Chop it with the spoon into crumbly bits.
3. Add the stock powder or cube, herbs, chilli, tomatoes and tomato cocktail, and stir well to combine.
4. Bring to the boil, then reduce the heat, cover and simmer over a low heat for 20–30 minutes, stirring occasionally. Add a little water, if necessary.
5. Add the kidney beans and heat through. Season to taste.
6. Serve with rice, pasta or in wraps.

SERVES 2 (4)

COTTAGE PIE

1 Tbsp oil
1 onion, peeled and chopped
1 clove garlic, peeled and finely chopped
500 g lean beef mince
1 Tbsp gravy powder
1 tsp beef stock powder or 1 stock cube
1 cup water
1 tsp dried mixed herbs
1 Tbsp Worcestershire sauce
a squirt of tomato sauce
salt and pepper to taste

TOPPING
3 large potatoes
a thick slice of butter
a dash of milk
salt to taste

1. Heat the oil in a medium saucepan and fry the onion and garlic over a moderate heat for 3–4 minutes.
2. Add the mince and cook for 8–10 minutes, stirring continuously, until browned all over. Chop it with the spoon into crumbly bits.
3. Mix the gravy powder and stock powder or cube with the water. Stir this into the mince, and then add the herbs, Worcestershire sauce and tomato sauce. Season to taste.
4. Mix well and bring to the boil, then reduce the heat to low, cover and simmer for 30 minutes, giving an occasional stir to prevent the mince from sticking to the pan.
5. Meanwhile, microwave the potatoes for 10–12 minutes, then peel. Alternatively, peel, wash and cut the potatoes into small cubes and boil for 20 minutes in a pot of water until soft. Drain off the water.
6. Add the butter, milk and salt to the potatoes and mash until smooth.
7. Pour the mince into a serving dish and top with the mashed potato, using a fork to spread the mash evenly over the mince.

SERVES 2–3

BEEF STEAK WITH PESTO PASTA

This is another meal in one dish.

⅓ x 500 g pkt pasta
3 Tbsp pesto
1 Tbsp oil
250–300 g beef steak, cubed
1 clove garlic, peeled and finely chopped
1 chilli, finely chopped
garlic and herb seasoning
8 baby tomatoes, washed
a good handful of rocket leaves, washed
¼ cup shaved pecorino or any strong white cheese

1. Boil the pasta in salted water with a dash of oil for 12 minutes until tender, but firm. Drain and put into a large serving dish. Mix in the pesto and keep warm.
2. Heat the oil in a large frying pan over a moderate heat and add the beef, garlic, chilli and a sprinkle of garlic and herb seasoning. Stir-fry for 5–7 minutes until the meat is browned on the outside and pink on the inside.
3. Pour the meat and juices into the pasta and mix well.
4. Toss in the baby tomatoes, rocket and shaved cheese, and serve immediately.

SERVES 2

STIR-FRIED BEEF WITH BLACK BEAN SAUCE

1½ Tbsp oil
1 small onion, peeled and thinly sliced
1 clove garlic, peeled and finely chopped
300–350 g beef steak, thinly sliced
1 level tsp cornflour
2 tsp soy sauce
½ beef stock cube or 2 tsp stock powder
½ cup water
1 Tbsp black bean sauce

1. Heat half of the oil in a large frying pan over a moderate heat and fry the onion and garlic, stirring occasionally, for 4 minutes.
2. Push these to one side, turn up the heat and pour the remaining oil into the pan. Add the beef and stir-fry for 3–4 minutes to brown all over. Mix in the onion and garlic.
3. Remove the pan from the heat for a moment and reduce the heat to moderate.
4. Mix the cornflour with the soy sauce until smooth, then mix in the stock cube or powder and the water. Pour this into the pan.
5. Return the pan to the heat and stir while the sauce thickens slightly.
6. Stir in the black bean sauce and heat through.
7. Serve immediately with noodles or rice and stir-fried vegetables.

SERVES 2

BEEF STROGANOFF

1 Tbsp butter

1 Tbsp oil

1 small onion, peeled and sliced

125 g button mushrooms, washed and sliced

½ tsp garlic and herb salt

300 g beef steak, very thinly sliced

2 tsp soy sauce

½ cup thick sour cream

freshly ground black pepper to taste

1. Heat the butter and half of the oil in a large frying pan over a moderate heat and fry the onion for 3 minutes.
2. Add the mushrooms with the garlic and herb salt and stir-fry for 3–4 minutes.
3. Push the onion and mushroom mixture to one side of the pan, turn up the heat and add the remaining oil. Stir-fry the beef for 4–5 minutes so that it is still pink in the middle.
4. Mix the beef with the onion and mushroom mixture, and then stir in the soy sauce and sour cream. Heat through, season with black pepper and serve over rice or pasta.

TIPS - You can make any cream taste sour by adding a squirt of lemon juice.
- Do not double the butter and oil when doubling the recipe.

SERVES 2

BEEF IN GUINNESS
or stout

The amounts given in brackets are to help you double the recipe.

500 g stewing beef, trimmed and cubed (1 kg)

2 tsp cake flour (1 Tbsp)

salt and pepper to taste

2 Tbsp oil (3 Tbsp)

1 medium onion, peeled and chopped (1 large)

1 clove garlic, peeled and finely chopped (2 cloves)

2 carrots, peeled and sliced (4)

½ x 440 ml can Guinness/stout (1 x 440 ml can)

1 cup water (2 cups)

1 beef stock cube or 1 Tbsp stock powder (2 cubes or 2 Tbsp powder)

½ tsp dried thyme (1 tsp)

1. Put the beef into a bowl and cover with the flour and a little salt and pepper. Mix well to coat the beef evenly.
2. Heat 1 Tbsp of the oil in a large saucepan over a moderate heat and gently fry the onion, garlic and carrots for 5 minutes. Push to one side of the pan and turn up the heat.
3. Add the remaining oil and the beef, and stir to brown all over for 5–7 minutes, ensuring the beef doesn't stick to the bottom of the pan. Mix in the garlic and onion, and remove from the heat for a moment.
4. Open the Guinness or stout over the beef to catch the froth. Slowly pour in the beer over the back of a spoon, to reduce the froth. Mix well and stir in the water, stock cube or powder and thyme.
5. Return the pan to the heat, bring to the boil, and then reduce the heat to very low. Cover and simmer for about 2½ hours until the beef is tender and the sauce has reduced by half. Stir occasionally. Serve over fluffy mashed potato.

SERVES 2 (4)

THAI  SALAD

350–400 g beef steak
1½ Tbsp soy sauce
1 clove garlic, peeled and finely chopped
2 spring onions, trimmed and sliced (include a little of the dark green part)
1–2 red chillies, deseeded and finely chopped
1 tsp Thai fish sauce
1 tsp fresh lemon or lime juice
1 tsp sugar
2 Tbsp oil
mixed lettuce leaves
a handful of baby tomatoes
¼ English cucumber, cut into matchstick-like strips
a handful of fresh coriander leaves (optional)

1. Switch on the oven's grill.
2. Place the beef on an oven tray about 10 cm under the grill and cook for 5–7 minutes on each side, depending on how you like your steak done.
3. Thinly slice the cooked beef and put in a bowl. Pour over the soy sauce and mix.
4. Combine the garlic, spring onions, chillies, fish sauce, lemon or lime juice, sugar and oil in a cup. Add this to the beef, mixing in well.
5. Arrange the lettuce leaves with the tomatoes and cucumber on a platter and top with the beef. Garnish with coriander if desired.

SERVES 2

PORK

SAUSAGES IN TOMATO AND ONION SAUCE

This beautifully simple and tasty meal is a variation of a Mauritian dish, Rougail saucisses. When doubling, only increase the number of sausages. Leave all the other ingredients the same – there's plenty of sauce to go around.

2 Tbsp oil
4–6 large pork sausages
1 small onion, peeled and chopped
2 cloves garlic, peeled and chopped
1 x 400 g can Italian tomatoes
3–4 Tbsp sweet chilli sauce

1. Heat half of the oil in a medium frying pan over a moderate heat and fry the sausages for 10–15 minutes, turning to brown evenly and cook through. Remove the sausages from the pan and keep warm in a serving dish.
2. Discard the watery pan juices and rinse the pan.
3. Heat the remaining oil and gently fry the onion and garlic over a low heat for 5 minutes, then mash in the tomatoes and their juices.
4. Simmer for 5–7 minutes until the liquid has reduced a little.
5. Mix in the sweet chilli sauce and then pour over the sausages.
6. Serve immediately with mashed potato.

SERVES 2

PORK FILLET IN MUSTARD CREAM

2 tsp grain mustard

½ cup cream

½ cup strong chicken stock made with ½ chicken stock cube or 2 tsp stock powder and ½ cup water

250 g pork fillet, trimmed of membrane and thinly sliced

¼ tsp ground ginger

2 tsp soy sauce

1 Tbsp oil

salt and ground black pepper to taste

1. In a small jug, mix the mustard into the cream and stir in the stock. Set aside.
2. Put the pork in a bowl and sprinkle over the ginger and soy sauce. Turn the meat to cover it in the sauce.
3. Heat the oil in a medium frying pan over a high heat and stir-fry the pork for 3–4 minutes to brown all over.
4. Pour in the mustard cream and bring to the boil. Reduce the heat to low and gently simmer for 7–8 minutes to reduce the sauce and cook the meat through. Season to taste.
5. Serve with rice, noodles or mashed potato and vegetables.

Variation
Add 1 Tbsp green peppercorns to the mustard cream at the beginning.

SERVES 2

IN PEANUT SAUCE

250–300 g lean pork, cubed
2 tsp cake flour
salt and pepper to taste
1 Tbsp oil
1 clove garlic, peeled and finely chopped
1 small onion, peeled and chopped
2 Tbsp peanut butter
½ beef stock cube or 1 heaped tsp stock powder
1 cup water
1 Tbsp soy sauce
2 tsp sweet chilli sauce (optional)

1. Put the pork into a bowl and cover with the flour and a little salt and pepper. Mix well to coat the pork evenly.
2. Heat the oil in a large frying pan over a moderate heat and fry the garlic and onion for 5 minutes until soft.
3. Push the garlic and onion to one side, turn up the heat and stir-fry the pork for 5 minutes to brown all over. Mix in the garlic and onion, remove from the heat for a moment and turn down the heat to low.
4. Mix the peanut butter, stock cube or powder, water and soy sauce in a jug and pour onto the pork. Stir until the sauce thickens, return the pan to the heat and simmer gently for 10 minutes until the pork is cooked through.
5. Stir in the sweet chilli sauce if using (it gives the dish an interesting spicy flavour).
6. Serve with rice and vegetables.

SERVES 2

GAMMON STEAKS WITH PINEAPPLE

2 tsp wholegrain mustard
2 large gammon steaks
1 Tbsp oil
1 tsp butter
2 fresh or canned pineapple rings

1. Spread the mustard over both sides of the gammon steaks.
2. Heat the oil and butter in a frying pan over a moderate heat and fry the steaks for 5 minutes on each side. Stack on one side of the pan.
3. Add the pineapple rings to the pan and heat for 1 minute on both sides, covering them in the pan juices.
4. Serve the gammon with the pineapple rings on top and the pan juices poured over.

SERVES 2

STIR-FRIED PORK
WITH SWEET CHILLI SAUCE

250 g pork fillet, trimmed of membrane
and thinly sliced
1 Tbsp soy sauce
1 Tbsp sesame or cooking oil
½ small onion, peeled and sliced thinly
1 clove garlic, peeled and finely chopped
¼ tsp grated or powdered ginger
½ small red pepper, deseeded and cut
into thin strips
1 level tsp cornflour
½ beef stock cube or 2 tsp stock powder
½ cup water
1 Tbsp sweet chilli sauce

1. Put the pork into a bowl and pour over the soy sauce. Set aside.
2. Heat half of the oil in a large frying pan over a moderate heat and stir-fry the onion, garlic, ginger and red pepper for 5 minutes.
3. Push this mix to one side of the pan and turn up the heat. Add the remaining oil and the pork. Stir-fry to brown all over, and then stir in the onion mix. Remove the pan from the heat for a moment and turn down the heat to low.
4. Mix the cornflour and stock cube or powder with a little of the water to make a smooth paste. Stir in the remaining water and pour this into the pan. Return the pan to the heat, stirring continuously while the sauce thickens slightly.
5. Stir in the sweet chilli sauce and heat through.
6. Serve immediately with noodles or rice and stir-fried vegetables.

SERVES 2

LAMB

SPICY LAMB

Thread this lamb onto kebabs sticks or use to stuff warm pita pockets. Alternatively, serve on a bed of rice or noodles with vegetables.

400 g lamb, trimmed and cubed
1 x 175 ml tub plain yoghurt
2 cloves garlic, peeled and finely chopped
1 tsp powdered ginger or ½ tsp chopped fresh
1 tsp finely chopped chilli
salt and pepper to taste
juice of ½ lemon
1 Tbsp oil
wooden kebab sticks or 2 pita breads

1. Mix the lamb with the yoghurt, garlic, ginger, chilli, salt and pepper and half of the lemon juice. Leave to marinade for at least 30 minutes, preferably longer, or even overnight.
2. To barbecue lamb kebabs, thread the cubes onto wet wooden kebab sticks and cook over hot coals, turning once to cook evenly. Sprinkle with the remaining lemon juice before serving.
3. To fry the lamb for pitas, first drain off the marinade. Heat the oil in a frying pan over a fairly high heat and stir-fry the lamb cubes for 8–10 minutes, stirring to brown quickly all over. Sprinkle with the remaining lemon juice and serve in warm pita pockets with salad.

TIPS - Buy a jar of ready-combined chopped garlic, ginger and chilli from the supermarket to save time.
- Make your own kebab sticks from rosemary stems with the 'leaves' removed.

SERVES 2

CRISPY-COATED CHOPS

2 tsp cake flour
6 lamb rib chops, trimmed of excess fat
⅓ cup breadcrumbs (about 1 thick slice of bread)
2 cloves garlic, peeled and finely chopped
1 Tbsp chopped fresh parsley
2 tsp grated lemon rind (from 1 whole lemon)
salt to taste
1 egg, lightly beaten
1 Tbsp oil
1 Tbsp butter

1. Sprinkle the flour over both sides of the chops and shake off the excess to coat lightly.
2. Combine the breadcrumbs, garlic, parsley and lemon rind in a bowl, season with salt and mix well.
3. Dip the floured chops in the beaten egg and then in the breadcrumb mixture, generously coating both sides.
4. Heat the oil and butter in a large frying pan over a moderate heat and fry the coated chops for 4–5 minutes each side, turning down the heat if the breadcrumbs start to brown too quickly. The lamb should be slightly pink inside and the coating crispy.

SERVES 2

CURRIED LAMB

This is best made the day before to let the lamb soak up the flavour.

2 Tbsp oil
1 medium onion, peeled and sliced
1 tsp curry powder (for a mild curry)
1 tsp coriander seeds
1 clove garlic, peeled and finely chopped
450 g lamb (leg or shoulder), trimmed and cubed
1 x 400 g can Italian tomatoes
½ tsp sugar
1 cup water
salt to taste

1. In a large saucepan, heat half of the oil over a moderate heat and fry the onion for about 5 minutes until lightly browned.
2. Add the curry powder, coriander seeds and garlic, and gently fry for 1–2 minutes.
3. Add the remaining oil and the lamb. Stir-fry the meat for 5 minutes to brown all over and coat evenly with the spices.
4. Mash in the tomatoes, and then add the sugar, water and a little salt.
5. Put the lid on at an angle and simmer over a very low heat for about 1 hour until the lamb is tender and the sauce is reduced and thickened.
6. Serve with rice and chutney. Other bits and pieces that go well with this curry are diced cucumber in plain yoghurt, nuts, raisins and chopped apple.

TIPS
- The tastiness of curry depends on frying the spices for the right amount of time – just until you can smell the aroma and no longer, as burnt spices turn bitter.
- Do not double the oil, sugar and water when doubling the recipe.

SERVES 2

121

LAMB CHOPS
WITH TOMATO

1½ Tbsp oil
1 onion, peeled and chopped
1 clove garlic, peeled and finely chopped
6 lamb rib chops, trimmed of fat
garlic and herb seasoning
1 x 400 g can Italian tomatoes
½ tsp sugar
½ tsp dried origanum
2 tsp beef stock powder or ½ stock cube
½ cup water

1. Heat half of the oil in a large frying pan over a moderate heat
   and fry the onion and garlic for 3–4 minutes until soft.
   Push to one side of the pan and add the remaining oil.
2. Turn up the heat and add the chops.
   Sprinkle with a little garlic and herb seasoning and fry
   for 4 minutes on each side to brown. Mix in the onion and garlic.
3. Mash in the tomatoes and add the sugar, origanum,
   stock powder or cube and water. Mix and bring to the boil.
4. Reduce the heat, cover and simmer gently for 15 minutes.
5. Serve with mashed potato or noodles.

SERVES 2

LAMB HOT POT

This is a meal in one dish.

650 g lamb chops (this gives about 400 g lean meat)
1 Tbsp cake flour
salt to taste
1 Tbsp oil
1 medium onion, peeled and sliced
1 large carrot, peeled and sliced
2 tsp beef stock powder or 1 stock cube
1½ cups water
1 sprig fresh rosemary or 1 tsp dried mixed herbs
2 large potatoes, peeled and sliced
2 tsp butter

1. Preheat the oven to 180 °C.
2. Take the lean meat off the bones and cut into cubes. Sprinkle with flour and season with salt.
3. Heat the oil in a large frying pan over a moderate heat and fry the onion and carrot for 4 minutes. Make a space in the middle and add the lamb. Brown the meat all over for 5 minutes, and then transfer everything to an ovenproof dish.
4. Mix in the stock powder or cube, water and rosemary needles or mixed herbs.
5. Boil the potato slices for 5 minutes in a pot of water, drain and shake in a sieve to flake slightly. Layer the potatoes on top of the lamb, overlapping the slices. Roughly spread the butter over the potatoes.
6. Cover with a lid or foil and bake in the centre of the oven for 1½ hours. If the dish is full, put a baking tray underneath to catch any spillage.
7. Uncover and turn up the heat to 220 °C. Bake for a further 30 minutes to brown the potatoes or speed up the process under the grill.

SERVES 2

BRAIN FOOD

CREAMY CURRIED HAKE

1 Tbsp oil

1 Tbsp butter

1 small onion, peeled and finely chopped

1 clove garlic, peeled and finely chopped

1 tsp cake flour

1 tsp curry powder

1 cup cream

2 tsp tomato purée

a squirt of lemon juice

300–400 g fresh hake, washed and cut into fairly large cubes

salt and pepper to taste

1. In a medium saucepan, heat the oil and butter over a moderate heat and gently cook the onion and garlic for 3–4 minutes, stirring occasionally, until soft.
2. Add the flour and curry powder, stirring for 2 minutes until fragrant.
3. Pour in the cream and stir while the sauce heats and thickens.
4. Mix in the tomato purée and lemon juice.
5. Add the hake and simmer over a very low heat for 10 minutes. Season to taste.
6. Serve with rice, diced tomato, onion and cucumber.

TIP Add cooked shrimps to the pot for extra luxury or use prawns instead of hake for a special occasion.

SERVES 2

TUNA AND SWEETCORN BAKE

This is delicious served with a crisp salad.

1 x 170 g can tuna
½ x 420 g can cream-style sweetcorn
2 eggs, beaten
salt and pepper to taste
½ cup grated cheese

1. Preheat the oven to 180 °C. Grease an ovenproof dish with a little oil.
2. In a bowl, mix the tuna, sweetcorn and eggs, and season to taste.
3. Pour the tuna mixture into the greased dish and sprinkle the cheese on top.
4. Bake for 30 minutes.

SERVES 2

IN BEER BATTER

½ cup cake flour
salt and pepper to taste
½–¾ cup chilled lager beer
2 firm white fish fillets
1 cup oil

1. Sift the flour into a bowl and season with salt and pepper. Whisk in the beer to make a smooth batter the consistency of thick pouring cream.
2. Shake a little extra flour over the fish, and then dip the fillets in the batter.
3. Heat the oil in a frying pan over a moderate heat. When sizzling (use a tiny drop of batter to test), add the fish and cook for 4–5 minutes until crisp and golden.
4. Remove and drain on paper towels. Serve immediately with lemon wedges or tartare sauce (see page 47).

SERVES 2

SPICY FISH CAKES

300 g firm white fish, finely chopped or 250 g fish
   and ½ cup cooked shrimps

1 egg

2 spring onions, trimmed and sliced

1 clove garlic, peeled and finely chopped

1 chilli, deseeded and finely chopped

1 slice bread, crusts removed and torn into pieces

2 tsp lemon juice

2 tsp fish sauce

1–2 Tbsp oil

1. Blitz everything except the oil in a blender for a few seconds.
   The mixture should be quite chunky. Alternatively, mix all the
   ingredients in a bowl.
2. Use 2 dessertspoons to lift out the mixture and shape it into 6 patties.
3. Heat 1 Tbsp oil in a large frying pan over a moderate heat and fry the patties together in a single
   layer for 4–5 minutes per side, adding a little more oil if needed.
4. Serve with lemon wedges and tartare sauce or coriander mayonnaise (see page 47).
   Alternatively, mix a little wasabi with mayonnaise for a hot dipping sauce.

SERVES 2 (MAKES 6)

BAKED FISH IN TOMATO AND PAPRIKA CREAM

300–400 g firm fish or 2 individual
   150–200 g fish fillets
½ cup cream
a squirt of lemon juice
½ cup canned chopped peeled tomatoes
   or 3 Tbsp tomato purée
1 tsp paprika
salt and pepper to taste
a few drops Tabasco (optional)
½ cup grated cheese

1. Preheat the oven to 180 °C. Lightly grease a baking dish with oil.
2. Place the fish in a single layer in the bottom of the dish.
3. Mix the cream, lemon juice, tomatoes or tomato purée and paprika, and season to taste. Add the Tabasco if using.
4. Spread the cream mixture over the fish and top with the grated cheese.
5. Bake uncovered for 20 minutes until the fish is just cooked through.

SERVES 2

GRILLED FISH FILLETS

2 firm fish fillets, roughly 200 g each
1 Tbsp oil
juice of ½ lemon
sprinkle of fish spice or dried thyme (optional)

1. Preheat the oven's grill. Line a grill pan with foil (this will keep the fish moist and will save you time washing up later).
2. Place the fish on the grill pan, cover with the oil and half of the lemon juice, and sprinkle with fish spice or dried thyme, if desired.
3. Place under the grill for 4–5 minutes, then turn and pour over the remaining lemon juice. Grill for a further 4–5 minutes, depending on the thickness of the fillets. If frozen, they may need longer. The fish is ready when it turns opaque and flakes easily.
4. Serve plain or with any of the following:
   lemon butter (melted butter with lemon juice added);
   garlic butter (melted butter with crushed garlic added);
   mayonnaise mixed with a little anchovy paste;
   or any sauce of your choice (see pages 46–47).

SERVES 2

THAI FISH STEW

The amounts given in brackets are to help you double the recipe.

1 cup coconut milk (2 x 400 ml cans)
150 g firm white fish, cut into fairly large cubes (400 g)
300 g frozen mixed seafood (600 g)
½ cup fish/chicken/vegetable stock (½ cup)
½ tsp ground ginger (1 tsp)
1 tsp chopped red chilli (2 tsp)
2 spring onions, trimmed and sliced (4)
1 Tbsp Thai fish sauce (2 Tbsp)
1½ Tbsp fresh lime or lemon juice (3 Tbsp)
a handful of fresh coriander, washed and destalked (do not chop)

1. Heat the coconut milk in a large saucepan over a moderate heat and, when just starting to bubble, add the fish, mixed seafood, stock and ginger.
2. Bring to the boil and then reduce the heat to very low. Simmer gently for 7 minutes.
3. Add the chilli and spring onions and cook for a further 2 minutes.
4. Remove from the heat and stir in the fish sauce, lime or lemon juice and most of the coriander.
5. Garnish with the remaining coriander before serving with rice.

SERVES 2–3 (4–6)

MIXED SEAFOOD PASTA

⅓ x 500 g pkt spaghetti
1 Tbsp oil
1 small onion, peeled and chopped
2 cloves garlic, peeled and chopped
1 x 400 g can Italian tomatoes
1 red chilli, deseeded and chopped (optional)
1 tsp chopped fresh basil
1 tsp lemon juice
½ tsp sugar
300–400 g frozen mixed seafood, thawed
salt and pepper to taste

1. Cook the spaghetti according to the instructions on page 57. It should be al dente. Put the cooked spaghetti into a large warm serving dish and set aside.
2. Heat the oil in a large frying pan over a moderate heat and fry the onion and garlic for 4 minutes until soft. Mash in the tomatoes and add the chilli (if using), basil, lemon juice and sugar.
3. Simmer over a low heat for 5 minutes, and then add the seafood. Cover and simmer for a further 5 minutes until the seafood is just cooked. Overcooking seafood makes it tough, so watch it. Season to taste.
4. Mix the sauce into the spaghetti and serve immediately.

 Use boiling water from the kettle to save energy.

SERVES 2–3

CALAMARI STEAKS WITH MOZZARELLA AND PESTO

Seafood makes wonderful dishes. It can be easily found in most shops, displayed in dedicated upright freezers.

This only takes about 10 minutes in total to make.

2 x 150–200 g frozen calamari steaks, rinsed and thawed
1 tsp butter
4–6 slices mozzarella cheese
2 tsp pesto

1. Preheat the oven's grill.
2. Place the calamari steaks in an ovenproof dish, spread with the butter and grill, close to the heat, on one side for 2–3 minutes.
3. Turn over the steaks, cover with the cheese and spread 1 tsp pesto on each.
4. Grill for 3 minutes until golden and bubbling.
5. Serve immediately with rice.

SERVES 2

CALAMARI IN GARLIC AND LEMON BUTTER SAUCE

This sauce also goes well with cooked prawns.

1½ Tbsp lemon juice
2½ cloves garlic, peeled and finely chopped
1 cup cubed cold butter (dice size)
1 Tbsp oil
300–400 g calamari nuggets or rings
salt and pepper to taste

1. Heat the lemon juice and garlic in a small saucepan over a moderate heat.
2. Reduce the heat to low and whisk in the butter, 3 or 4 cubes at a time. The sauce will thicken to a creamy consistency in 6–7 minutes. Remove the pan from the heat and set aside.
3. Heat the oil in a large frying pan over a fairly high heat and add the calamari. Season with salt and pepper, and stir-fry for 3–4 minutes until cooked through.
4. Spoon the calamari into a serving dish and drizzle over the sauce. Serve with plain or fried rice.

SERVES 2

CALAMARI SALAD

½ x 180 g pkt mixed leaf salad or ½ lettuce head, chopped
1 large carrot, peeled and grated
8 baby tomatoes, halved
2 spring onions, trimmed and sliced
a few slices of cucumber
2 x 150–200 g frozen calamari steaks, rinsed in hot water to thaw
2 Tbsp lemon juice
garlic and herb seasoning

DRESSING
1 Tbsp mayonnaise
2 Tbsp lemon juice
1 chilli, deseeded and finely chopped
salt and pepper to taste

1. Assemble the salad by placing the lettuce, carrot, tomatoes, spring onions and cucumber on a plate.
2. Slice the calamari steaks into thin strips, and then stir-fry them in the lemon juice with the garlic and herb seasoning for 3–4 minutes. Transfer from the pan to a small dish.
3. Mix the dressing ingredients and pour over the calamari. Toss to coat the calamari in the dressing before spooning onto the salad. Pour over any extra dressing.

SERVES 2

BRAIN FOOD

SEAFOOD WITH RICE

This is a variation on Spanish paella, without the yellow saffron, which is the most expensive spice on Earth!
It's an impressive meal in one pan that goes far if you want to entertain a few friends.

1 Tbsp oil
1 tsp butter
1 small onion, peeled and chopped
1 clove garlic, peeled and finely chopped
1 small red pepper, deseeded and diced
¾ cup white rice, rinsed in a sieve
1½ cups water
1 chicken stock cube or 1 Tbsp stock powder
½ cup frozen peas, rinsed in boiling water to thaw
300 g frozen mixed seafood, rinsed and thawed
200 g frozen mussels in half shells, rinsed and thawed
salt and pepper to taste
a sprinkle of paprika (optional)
1 lemon, cut into wedges

1. Heat the oil and butter in a large frying pan over a moderate heat and fry the onion, garlic and red pepper for 3–4 minutes.
2. Mix in the rice, stirring to coat in the buttery mixture for 1 minute.
3. Pour in the water with the stock cube or powder, ensuring the rice is well covered. Bring to the boil, and then reduce the heat to fairly low. Cover the pan and simmer gently for 10 minutes.
4. Add the peas, mixed seafood and mussels evenly on top, without stirring. Cover and cook for a further 5–7 minutes, until the rice is tender and the liquid is absorbed.
5. Season to taste and sprinkle with paprika, if using.
6. Using 1 or 2 lemon wedges, squeeze a little lemon juice over the seafood. Scatter the remaining wedges over the 'paella' and serve immediately straight from the pan.

Variation Add slices of fried chorizo to give the dish a spicy flavour.

SERVES 2–3

BERRY, NUT AND CHEESE SALAD

This takes 5 minutes to prepare!

½ x 180 g pkt mixed leaf salad
½ cup seedless grapes, rinsed
½ small red onion, peeled and thinly sliced
½ cup berries (such as gooseberries)
½ cup nuts, lightly toasted in a dry frying pan over low heat
¼ cup crumbly cheese (such as feta)

DRESSING
1 tsp Dijon or grain mustard
1 tsp honey
a pinch of salt and ground black pepper
1 Tbsp white balsamic vinegar
2 Tbsp oil

1. Shake all of the dressing ingredients together in a sealed jar.
2. Assemble the salad by placing the mixed lettuce leaves on a platter. Scatter the grapes, onion slices, berries and nuts over the lettuce and crumble the cheese on top.
3. Drizzle the dressing over the salad or serve separately in a jug.

SERVES 2

To serve crisp salad, wash your greens in sugared ice-cold water. This will freshen up any wilted lettuce. Where a recipe suggests a 180 g packet of mixed leaf salad, you can use half an iceberg lettuce instead, or any other type of salad greens.

AVOCADO SALSA

1 large avocado, peeled and cubed or mashed
1 tomato, cubed
1 spring onion, trimmed and sliced
1 small chilli, finely chopped (optional)

1 tsp garlic and herb seasoning
a handful of fresh coriander, destalked
  and chopped
1 Tbsp lemon juice

1. Gently mix all of the salsa ingredients in a serving bowl and sprinkle with the lemon juice.
2. Serve with meat, fish or as a stand-alone side dish.

SERVES 2

MiXeD BeAN SaLaD

a handful of green beans, washed, topped and tailed
½ x 400 g can mixed
   beans, rinsed in a sieve

DRESSING
1 tsp grain mustard
1 clove garlic, peeled and
   finely chopped
½ tsp sugar
1 Tbsp balsamic vinegar
2 Tbsp oil
salt and pepper to taste

1. Boil the green beans in
   a pot of water for
   4 minutes. Drain and
   rinse in cold water
   before arranging on a
   serving plate.
2. Mix all of the dressing
   ingredients in a bowl
   and add the mixed
   beans to marinade for
   a few minutes.
3. Pour this mixture over
   the green beans and
   gently toss.

SERVES 2–3

CARROT AND ALMOND SALAD

3 Tbsp flaked almonds

2 tsp mixed seeds

2–3 large carrots, peeled, washed and grated

a handful of fresh coriander leaves, washed and destalked

DRESSING

3 Tbsp oil

1 Tbsp lemon juice

1 tsp garlic and herb seasoning

½ tsp ground cumin

1. Lightly toast the almonds and seeds in a dry frying pan over a low heat for 5 minutes, shaking the pan to toast them evenly. Set aside in a small bowl.
2. Put the grated carrots, almonds, seeds and coriander in a mixing bowl and mix well.
3. Shake all of the dressing ingredients together in a sealed jar.
4. Pour the dressing over the carrot salad and gently toss.

SERVES 2–4

SPINACH SALAD

2 Tbsp oil
4 rashers bacon
2 slices bread or 3 slices French loaf
100 g baby spinach leaves, washed and dried
2 spring onions, trimmed and sliced

DRESSING
2 tsp balsamic vinegar
1 tsp grain mustard
½ tsp chopped garlic
½ tsp sugar
2 Tbsp oil

1. Heat 1 Tbsp oil in a frying pan and fry the bacon on both sides until brown and crispy. Remove and chop into bits, then set aside.
2. Add the remaining oil to the pan. Tear the bread into small pieces and fry, turning constantly, until brown all over. Don't be tempted to add more oil as this will make the fried bread greasy.
3. Arrange the spinach leaves in a serving dish and scatter over the spring onions.
4. Mix the dressing ingredients and pour over the spinach.
5. Sprinkle the bacon and bread over the salad and toss lightly.

SERVES 2

SUNSET SALAD

	DRESSING
½ x 180 g pkt mixed leaf salad	1½ tsp lemon juice
8 baby tomatoes, halved	1 tsp honey
1 large or 2 medium carrots, peeled and grated	1 tsp grain mustard
2 cups cubed watermelon	2 tsp chopped fresh mint
½ cup cubed feta cheese	1½ Tbsp oil

1. Shake all of the dressing ingredients together in a sealed jar.
2. Make a bed of lettuce on a serving dish and cover with the tomatoes, carrots and watermelon.
3. Crumble the feta on top and pour over the dressing.

SERVES 2

SWEETCORN SOUFFLÉ

2 tsp oil	½ x 420 g can cream-style sweetcorn
½ small onion, peeled and chopped	1 cup grated Cheddar cheese
2 eggs	salt and pepper to taste

1. Preheat the oven to 180 °C. Lightly grease an ovenproof dish with a little oil.
2. Heat the oil in a small frying pan and fry the onion over a low heat for 5 minutes.
3. In a bowl, mix the eggs, sweetcorn, fried onion and ½ cup cheese. Season to taste.
4. Pour the egg mixture into the dish and sprinkle the remaining cheese on top.
5. Bake for 30 minutes and serve hot.

SERVES 2

POTATO SALAD

10 baby potatoes, washed
salt and pepper to taste
2 spring onions, trimmed and sliced
2 Tbsp chopped fresh parsley

DRESSING
2 tsp white vinegar
1 tsp chopped garlic
3 Tbsp mayonnaise
1 Tbsp plain yoghurt

1. Boil the potatoes in a pot of water for 15–20 minutes until soft, but still firm. Rinse with cold water, cut in half and put in a serving dish. Season with salt and pepper and add the spring onions.
2. Combine the dressing ingredients in a small bowl and gently mix into the potatoes. Sprinkle the parsley on top before serving.

SERVES 2

CHEESY BROCCOLI

½ quantity cheese sauce (see page 46)
water for boiling
½ head broccoli, cut into florets and washed

1. Make the cheese sauce and keep it warm in the saucepan.
2. Fill a small saucepan about a quarter-full with water and bring to the boil over a fairly high heat. Add the broccoli, half cover with the lid and boil for about 7 minutes until tender and still firm. Drain and put into a serving dish.
3. Pour the cheese sauce over the top and serve.

SERVES 2

TOMATO AND MOZZARELLA SALAD

2 ripe tomatoes, sliced

6 slices mozzarella cheese

2 tsp chopped fresh basil

1 small carrot, peeled and cut into matchsticks

1 stick celery, cut into matchsticks

DRESSING

¼ tsp English mustard

½ tsp sugar

pinch of salt and ground black pepper

1 tsp balsamic vinegar

1 Tbsp oil

1. Arrange the tomatoes and cheese in a dish, alternating and overlapping them.
2. Scatter over the basil, carrot and celery.
3. Mix the dressing ingredients in a small bowl and drizzle over the salad.

SERVES 2

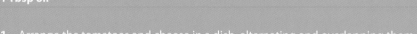

STEAMED VEGETABLES

You start by stir-frying the vegetables in a little oil to bring out the best flavour, and then you cook them in their own juices. When cooked, the vegetables should still be firm.

1 Tbsp sesame or vegetable oil
2 tsp soy sauce

CHOOSE A SELECTION OF COLOURFUL VEGETABLES OR USE THEM ALL:
1 carrot, peeled and cut into thin strips
1 leek, washed and thinly sliced lengthways
4 baby sweetcorn, cut in half lengthways
2 courgettes, washed and cut into long strips
4 small broccoli florets
½ small red pepper, deseeded and cut into long strips
a handful of sugar snap peas, topped and tailed (to remove the strings down the sides)
a handful of bean sprouts, washed

1. Heat the oil in a large frying pan over a moderate heat. Add the carrot, leek, sweetcorn, courgettes, broccoli and red pepper, and stir-fry for 2 minutes. Add 1 tsp water.
2. Reduce the heat, cover the pan with a lid and steam the vegetables for 4 minutes, stirring once or twice.
3. Add the sugar snap peas and bean sprouts, and steam for a further 2 minutes.
4. Sprinkle the soy sauce over the vegetables and mix lightly. Serve immediately.

TIP If doubling this recipe, keep the amounts of oil and soy sauce the same.

SERVES 2–3

BUTTERNUT MASH

This is a rich version of butternut mash, and is unbelievably moreish. To save time, use a 250 g bag of pre-cut butternut.

1 small butternut, peeled, deseeded and cut into small cubes
1 Tbsp butter

2 tsp cream cheese
salt and pepper to taste

1. Place the butternut in a saucepan and cover with water. Bring to the boil and simmer over a moderate heat for 20 minutes, until soft. Drain, keeping the butternut in the warm saucepan.
2. Mash the butternut with the butter and cream cheese, and season to taste.

 To save electricity, microwave the butternut for 5–7 minutes in a covered bowl instead of boiling it on the stove.

SERVES 2

CREAMED SPINACH

½ quantity white sauce (see page 46)
1 Tbsp smooth cottage cheese (optional)

1 cup water
300 g spinach, washed well

1. Make the white sauce, mix in the cottage cheese (if using) and keep it warm in the saucepan.
2. Bring the water to the boil in a large saucepan over a moderate heat. Add the spinach, which will be piled up well above the water level, and boil for 4–5 minutes until wilted. As the quantity of spinach reduces, gently stir. Remove from the heat and drain well. Roughly chop the spinach.
3. Mix the spinach with the sauce and serve immediately.

SERVES 2

ROAST VEGETABLES

1 x 250 g pkt prepared mixed vegetables for roasting

OR

½ butternut, peeled, deseeded and cubed

½ red pepper, washed, deseeded and sliced

3 courgettes, washed and halved lengthways

a handful of broccoli florets, washed

4 baby sweetcorn, washed and halved lengthways

1 small onion, peeled and quartered

1–2 Tbsp oil

garlic and herb salt to taste

1. Preheat the oven to 180 °C.
2. Put all of the vegetables in a roasting pan and spread evenly.
3. Drizzle over the oil and season with garlic and herb salt.
4. Bake for 40 minutes, turning once after 20 minutes.

TIP You could also use peeled and cut parsnips, carrots, leeks, aubergines and cauliflower.

SERVES 2–4

RATATOUILLE

This is a versatile dish that goes well with meat or fish. For a vegetarian meal, mix it into cooked pasta, top with cheese and grill.

1 Tbsp oil
1 small onion, peeled and chopped
1 clove garlic, peeled and finely chopped
½ small red pepper, deseeded and chopped
3 courgettes, washed and sliced
3 baby corn, sliced
1 x 400 g can Italian tomatoes
1 tsp dried mixed herbs
2–3 fresh basil leaves, chopped (optional)
salt and pepper to taste

1. Heat the oil in a frying pan over a moderate heat and fry the onion and garlic for 3 minutes.
2. Add the red pepper, courgettes and corn, cover and steam for 4 minutes, stirring occasionally.
3. Mash in the tomatoes with their juices and add the herbs and basil.
4. Bring to the boil and then cover and simmer on a very low heat for 15–20 minutes, stirring occasionally. Season with salt and pepper.

SERVES 2–3

GUILTY PLEASURES

HOT FRUIT CRUMBLE

This is so easy and delicious that it shouldn't be restricted to dessert time. It makes a great breakfast, as well as an all-day snack.

1 x 410 g can peach slices, drained or any fresh fruit
¼ tsp ground cinnamon
6 Tbsp oats
2 Tbsp cake flour
45 g butter
3 Tbsp brown sugar (if using fresh fruit, add 1–2 extra Tbsp sugar)

1. Preheat the oven to 200 °C.
2. Place the drained peaches in a small shallow baking dish and sprinkle with the cinnamon. If using fresh fruit, sprinkle with the extra sugar, depending on how sour the fruit is. No extra liquid is needed, as the fruit makes its own juice.
3. Blitz the oats, flour, butter and sugar in a blender for a few seconds, keeping the mixture fairly chunky. Alternatively, rub the flour and butter together until it resembles fine breadcrumbs, and then mix in the oats and sugar.
4. Shake the oat mixture over the fruit, covering it in a thick, even layer.
5. Bake in the centre of the oven for 25 minutes until brown and bubbling.
6. Serve hot or cold, on its own or with custard, cream or ice cream.

SERVES 2

CHILLED LEMON TART

1 x 200 g pkt ginger biscuits
125 g butter, melted
¾ cup cream
¾ x 385 g can condensed milk
2 large lemons
mint leaves or lemon slices for decoration (optional)

1. Crush the ginger biscuits into crumbs, either in a blender or with a rolling pin. Put the crumbs in a mixing bowl and mix in the melted butter.
2. Using the back of a spoon, press the biscuit mix into a 24 cm flan dish, covering the base and sides. Chill in the fridge until needed.
3. Meanwhile, make the filling. In a large mixing bowl, whip the cream until thick, and then whip in the condensed milk.
4. Finely grate the rind of 1 lemon into the cream mixture, before cutting both the lemons in half and squeezing in all the juice.
5. Slowly beat the lemon juice into the cream until the mixture begins to thicken.
6. Pour the lemon cream mixture onto the biscuit base and chill in the fridge for at least 3 hours until set.
7. Decorate with mint leaves or lemon slices if desired.

TIP Use a brush to get the lemon rind off the sharp teeth of the grater.

SERVES 6–8

PEACHES WITH HONEY CREAM YOGHURT

*This is also delicious made with sliced fresh
mangoes instead of the canned peaches.*

1 x 410 g can peach slices, drained
½ cup fresh cream
1 x 175 ml tub thick Greek yoghurt
1 Tbsp honey
1 Tbsp brown sugar

1. Place the peaches in the base of a serving dish.
2. Whip the cream and fold in the yoghurt.
3. Cover the fruit with the cream mixture, drizzle over the
   honey and sprinkle with the brown sugar.
4. Chill in the fridge for at least 1 hour.

SERVES 2

FRUIT WITH DIPPING CHOCOLATE

CHOOSE YOUR FAVOURITE FRUITS – HERE ARE SOME THAT GO WELL WITH CHOCOLATE:

strawberries, washed (leave stalks on)
pineapple, peeled and sliced
oranges, peeled and sliced
pears, peeled and sliced
bananas, peeled and sliced
apples, peeled and sliced (sprinkle with lemon juice to prevent discolouring)

DIP
90 g dark chocolate
½ cup cream

1. Arrange the fruits on a plate.
2. Break the chocolate into a small saucepan, add the cream and melt over a moderate heat, stirring until smooth.
3. Pour the chocolate dip into a small bowl and serve with your selection of fruits.

SERVES 2

162 GUILTY PLEASURES

BAR ONE/MARS BAR ICE CREAM

After freezing this overnight, it becomes like a semi-frozen fluffy mousse that melts fast. If you leave it longer in the freezer, it becomes a more solid ice cream … It just depends on your preference.

2 x 55 g Bar One/Mars Bar chocolate bars
90 g dark chocolate
1½ cups cream
2 eggs

1. Break the chocolate bars and dark chocolate into a saucepan and add ½ cup cream. Melt over a gentle heat and whisk well until smooth. Remove from the heat.
2. Crack 1 egg, pouring the white into a mixing bowl and the yolk into the chocolate mixture. Whisk in the yolk, then repeat for the second egg. Allow the mixture to cool.
3. Meanwhile, beat the egg whites until stiff.
4. Fold the chocolate mixture into the egg whites.
5. Whip the remaining cream into peaks and fold into the mixture.
6. Pour into a small loaf tin (about 20 x 9 cm) or serving dish. Cover with clingfilm and freeze for several hours.

SERVES 6–8

PAVLOVA

This is a wonderfully simple, cheap and impressive dessert to make for a party.
It is a good idea to make the pavlova in the evening, so that you can cook it on a low heat,
then turn the oven off and leave it to dry out overnight in the cooling oven.

4 egg whites	**2 tsp cornflour**
a pinch of salt	**1 cup cream**
1 cup castor sugar	**fresh fruit (berries are good)**

1. Preheat the oven to 130 °C. Grease a baking sheet with a little oil.
2. Beat the egg whites with the salt until stiff. Gradually add the sugar, one spoonful at a time, beating after each addition for a few minutes. The glossy mixture must form stiff peaks that hold their shape, even if you turn the bowl upside down! Fold in the cornflour.
3. Spoon the mixture in one big dollop onto the centre of the greased baking sheet. With the back of a spoon, spread it out into a circle or rectangle, pressing down from the centre outwards, to give a raised swirling border all round. The circle should be about 25 cm in diameter, allowing a bit of room at the edge of the baking sheet for the meringue to spread slightly.
4. Bake in the middle of the oven for 1½ hours, then turn off the heat and leave the meringue in the oven to dry out for several hours. (This will keep for ages in a sealed bag until you need it.)
5. When ready to serve, whip the cream into peaks and spoon into the meringue shell. Arrange the fruit on top and sift over some icing sugar before serving.

SERVES 6–8

Variations

Make a lemon cream filling: In a heatproof bowl, whisk 4 egg yolks with 4 Tbsp castor sugar for 1 minute. Whisk in 4 Tbsp lemon juice and the grated rind of 1 lemon. Stir over a pot of boiling water for 12–15 minutes until the eggs thicken. Remove from the heat and allow to cool. Whip ½ cup cream and fold in the lemon mixture. Chill until ready to use.

To make individual meringues, simply preheat the oven to 120 °C. Make the mixture as per the pavlova recipe and spoon dollops onto the greased baking sheet, leaving a little space in between each. Bake in the middle of the oven for 90 minutes, then turn off the heat and leave the meringues to dry out in the oven overnight. They keep for ages in a sealed container or plastic bag, so you can make them well in advance.

CHOCOLATE MOUSSE

You can make a party-size quantity of this by allowing about 30 g chocolate, 1 tsp water and 1 egg per person. Use a shallow dish.

60 g dark chocolate
2 tsp cold water
2 eggs

1. Bring a small amount of water (about 1 cup) to the boil in a saucepan, and then reduce to a slow simmer over a low heat.
2. Break the chocolate into a heatproof bowl that fits on top of the saucepan. Add the cold water and melt the chocolate over the saucepan of boiling water, stirring continuously as it starts to melt.
3. Crack open 1 egg, pour the white into a mixing bowl and the yolk into the melted chocolate. Stir in the yolk until it thickens slightly, then repeat with the remaining egg.
4. Remove the bowl from the heat and allow the chocolate mixture to cool.
5. Meanwhile, beat the egg whites until peaks form.
6. Gently fold the cooled chocolate mixture into the egg whites. Be careful not to over mix, as the mixture won't set properly if it is too liquid.
7. Pour the mixture into a serving dish or individual glasses and allow to set in the fridge for at least 4 hours.

SERVES 2

BASIC SPONGE CAKE

	BUTTER ICING
125 g butter	250 g soft butter
¾ cup milk	2 cups icing sugar, sifted
1 tsp vanilla essence	1 tsp vanilla essence
3 eggs	food colouring of choice (optional)
1 cup sugar	
1½ cups cake flour	
2 tsp baking powder	

1. Preheat the oven to 180 °C. Grease two 20 cm shallow round cake tins with a little oil. Cut out two circles of baking paper to fit in the base of the tins and line both. Lightly grease the paper with oil.
2. Melt the butter, milk and vanilla essence in a medium saucepan over a moderate heat.
3. In a large mixing bowl, beat the eggs until fluffy. Gradually add the sugar while still beating.
4. Hold a sieve over the bowl and sift the flour and baking powder into the egg mixture and then fold in gently.
5. Add the melted butter mixture and combine well.
6. Divide the batter between the two cake tins and bake for 15 minutes. Test they are ready by inserting a skewer or toothpick into the centre of each cake, which should come out clean. When done, take the cakes out of the oven and allow to cool in the tins for 5 minutes. Then turn them out onto a rack, remove the paper lining and allow to cool completely.
7. Make the icing by beating the butter with the icing sugar until pale and creamy. Mix in the vanilla essence and a few drops of food colouring if desired.
8. Use the icing to sandwich the two cooled cakes together and for icing the top.

Variation

Spread a layer of strawberry jam on the flat side of one cake, then add a layer of whipped cream. Cover with the other cake, flat-side down, and dust with sifted icing sugar. Slice and serve. You could even add in a layer of sliced strawberries between the jam and the cream and decorate the top with extra strawberries.

CHOCOLATE CAKE

This is a lovely moist cake that goes a long way. It is ideal for parties or celebrations, and is very quick and easy to make.

2 cups cake flour	**CHOCOLATE BUTTER ICING**
¾ cup cocoa powder	60 g soft butter
2 tsp bicarbonate of soda	2 cups icing sugar, sifted
1 tsp baking powder	2 Tbsp cocoa powder
½ tsp salt	2 Tbsp hot water
2 cups sugar	2 tsp vanilla essence
1 cup milk	
2 eggs	
½ cup oil	
1 cup strong coffee	

1. Preheat the oven to 180 °C. Grease a 24–26 cm cake tin (for a large single-layer cake) or two 22 cm round cake tins (for a smaller double-layer cake) with a little oil. Lightly dust with flour.
2. Sift the flour, cocoa powder, bicarbonate of soda, baking powder and salt into a large mixing bowl.
3. Add the remaining ingredients and mix well.
4. Pour the batter into the cake tin(s) and bake in the middle of the oven: 40–45 minutes for a large cake or 30–35 minutes for two smaller cakes.
5. Test they are ready by inserting a skewer or toothpick into the centre of each cake, which should come out clean. When done, take the cakes out of the oven and allow to cool in the tins for 5 minutes. Then turn them out onto a rack and allow to cool completely.
6. To make the icing, beat the butter with the icing sugar using a fork.
7. In a separate bowl, mix the cocoa powder with the water and vanilla essence until you have a smooth paste.
8. Add the cocoa mixture to the butter and icing sugar and mix until creamy.
9. Use this to sandwich the two cooled cakes together and for icing the top. Otherwise spread all of it over the top of the larger cooled cake.

Variation

Instead of butter icing, make this easy ganache: Melt together 180 g dark chocolate and ½ cup cream. Stir until smooth, allow to cool and pour over the cake.

CUPCAKES

125 g soft butter	**BUTTER ICING**
½ cup castor sugar	**1 cup icing sugar, sifted**
2 eggs	**125 g soft butter**
1 cup self-raising flour	**½ tsp vanilla essence**
¼ cup milk	**a few drops food colouring (optional)**
½ tsp vanilla essence	

1. Preheat the oven to 200 °C. Line a muffin pan with cupcake cases.
2. Beat the butter and sugar until creamy, and then beat in the eggs, one at a time.
3. Beat in half of the flour with half of the milk, and then add the remaining flour and milk, together with the vanilla essence. Beat until smooth.
4. Spoon into the cupcake cases, smoothing over the tops.
5. Bake in the centre of the oven for 15 minutes. Test to see if they are done by pressing their tops. They should be firm and spongy. Remove from the muffin pan and allow to cool on a rack.
6. To make the icing, beat the sugar, butter and vanilla essence until smooth and creamy. Mix in the food colouring, if using. This makes a generous amount of soft butter icing.
7. Spread or pipe a good dollop of icing on top of each cooled cupcake.
8. Decorate with rose petals, strawberries, blueberries, jellybeans or anything that takes your fancy.

TIP If you don't have a piping bag with shaped nozzles, improvise – put the icing into a plastic food bag and snip off one small corner. Twist the top closed and place the open corner over a cupcake. Squeeze the mixture out in circles ending with a point, like a soft-serve ice cream cone.

MAKES 12

CHOCOLATE BROWNIES

These are deliciously rich.

180 g dark chocolate with nuts
125 g butter
2 eggs
½ cup castor sugar
1 Tbsp strong black cold coffee
1 tsp vanilla essence
4 rounded Tbsp cake flour
a pinch of salt
icing sugar for dusting

1. Preheat the oven to 180 °C.
2. Grease a 22 cm-square baking tin with a little butter and line with baking paper.
3. Break the chocolate into a medium-sized heatproof bowl. Slice the butter and add to the chocolate. Either melt in the microwave for 1–1½ minutes or melt over a small saucepan of simmering water, stirring until smooth. Remove from the heat and allow to cool.
4. In a large mixing bowl, beat the eggs, sugar and coffee until creamy. Stir in the cooled chocolate and vanilla essence. Sift the flour and salt into the mixture and fold in gently.
5. Pour into the baking tin and bake in the centre of the oven for 30 minutes. Test to see if it's done by pressing lightly on top – it should be just set.
6. Allow to cool and cut into squares. Sift over some icing sugar just before serving.

TIP Don't overbeat or overcook. The brownie mixture will dry out.

MAKES 16

QUICK MICROWAVE CHOCOLATE CAKE

This is so incredible for instant entertaining that everyone will be impressed!

1 cup self-raising flour
1 tsp baking powder
1 cup castor sugar
4 Tbsp cocoa powder
½ cup milk
45 g soft butter
2 eggs
1 tsp vanilla essence

ICING
180 g dark chocolate
½ cup cream

1. Lightly grease a large plastic or silicon ring mould or round baking dish with a glass in the middle (no metal) with a little butter.
2. Beat all of the ingredients in a large mixing bowl, preferably with an electric beater, for 2 minutes until smooth and slightly pale in colour.
3. Pour into the greased mould or dish and microwave on full power for 5–6 minutes. Test to see if it is done by inserting a skewer or toothpick into the centre, which should come out clean.
4. Allow to cool for 5 minutes, and then turn the cake out onto a rack.
5. To make the icing, break the chocolate into a bowl and add the cream. Microwave for 1 minute to melt the chocolate. Alternatively, melt the chocolate and cream in a small saucepan over a moderate heat. Stir well until smooth.
6. Allow the icing to cool before pouring it over the cooled cake.

INDEX

Entries in bold indicate photographs